THE I AM MINDSET

Sheryl Smikle-Russell

For more information, address:
Becomingshe.me@gmail.com

First paperback edition November 2021

ISBN: 9798498303741

www.ssrlifecoaching.com

Table of Contents

Introduction

Have you ever asked yourself the questions –Who am I? What is my purpose for being here? Have you ever felt like you had no power or control over your life and believed that your circumstances were hopeless? Unfortunately, if you said yes to either of those questions, you are not alone.

So, please, let me introduce you to the concept of "The I AM Mindset." Countless people can relate to periods in their lives when this self-questioning and struggle with the feeling of hopelessness appeared to be the norm; if you are here and are willing to explore a new and empowering mindset, welcome!

I've written this book to guide you on a journey of self-empowerment as you contemplate your next steps in discovering or rediscovering who you are and your purpose for being here. This book is for you. Are you ready to focus on holding yourself accountable for your thoughts, emotions, and actions?

Life can be challenging when faced with responsibilities like self-care while raising a family, choosing a career/educational path, choosing, or moving on from a relationship–with a particular emphasis on women of color and indigenous women who may face additional obstacles while making these decisions.

As we begin, let's explore the words "I AM," which stands for Inspiring, Aspiring, and Motivating. These three words are the core of "The I AM Mindset" and are vital to experiencing The I AM Mindset philosophy.

- We need to figure out how to be inspired and Inspiring to ourselves and others.
- We need aspirations to aspire and be Aspiring.
- We need to be motivated and motivate or be Motivating.

I created this step-by-step self-empowerment book that's also a workbook. This book will serve you as a guide in figuring out what questions to ask yourself as I did when I came face-to-face with many challenging aspects of being a woman of color, an immigrant, and a person driven to succeed in life. Although I was determined, I held myself accountable for my actions.

Approach each section with an open mind and treat it as a free space to jot down possible answers to these life questions. Go back and see how all the chapters build on one another as a personalized guide when you're finished.

I hope that this book will be an excellent resource for you as you set out on a journey on becoming Inspiring, Aspiring, and Motivating with "The I AM Mindset."

Chapter 1

Discovering Who I AM

"Each moment describes who you are and gives you the opportunity to decide if that's who you want to be."

– Unknown

At one time in our lives or another, we all will feel the need to discover or rediscover who we are. Sometimes it will arrive out of a need for greater clarity or self-awareness; other times, it may come out of necessity. Perhaps a traumatic event in our lives may force us to rethink our own identity. Maybe we question how we fit into our social groups — or even our own families. We may want to assess our strengths and weaknesses for future challenges or aspirations, but however we do so, we must do so with the *correct mindset.*

I was a skinny, petite, brown-skinned girl standing at the airport in Kingston, Jamaica waving goodbye to my family. I had my one entry visa in hand, $60 U.S. dollars in my purse, and I headed to America, "The land of opportunity and the place where dreams come true."

"The greatest challenge in life is discovering who you are... and the second greatest is being happy with what you find."
– Unknown

Even as a young girl with big Aspiration, I knew that if I wanted to achieve my goals in this world, I would have to do it with intention. I would have to find a way to be Inspiring, Aspiring, and do so in a Motivating way—and this is that story...

Am I ready to discover the truth about who I am?

This book may have come along at a place in your life where you are feeling stuck and overwhelmed, or maybe you find yourself questioning who you are and your purpose for being here.

We often tend to approach this self-questioning from a place of fear, shame, and self-doubt.

This self-questioning can be healthy, constructive, and empowering if the primary purpose is to gain self-awareness. Our responsibility is to ask ourselves the hard questions (get a full-length mirror!) – Who am I? - What is my purpose? - When will I focus on myself? Where should I position myself to elevate? - Why am I here? How do I discover who I truly am so that I may claim my purpose?

"Just because you feel lost doesn't mean that you are. Sometimes you just have to relax, breathe deep, and trust the path you're on." — Lalah Delia

You are an extraordinary being, and even though this self-questioning may be uncomfortable at times, it is necessary for the process of moving forward in a way that is authentic and rooted in the hidden power you possess. The answers to your questions may be unique, but you are not alone. Most of us can relate to this type of soul-searching. Many of us have been there, and it is okay!

THE I AM MINDSET is you with a higher set of standards that allow you to take a holistic approach to your view of yourself and your purpose in life. As a result, your thoughts about who you are and the goals you choose to pursue will be different. After embodying this new way of viewing yourself, you will begin to expect more from all aspects of your life, and accountability will be your new paradigm.

I AM Here:
Inspiring, Aspiring, and Motivating.
I AM aware of who I AM,
My inspirations ignite my imagination.
Aspirations flow from a solid foundation,
There are no limitations.
I inhale and exhale with great ambition.
My hopes, my dreams, and my determination
move me to a higher elevation.
My motivations start with a passion.
I determine my actions and reactions.
I AM on a journey filled with satisfaction
Inspiration, Aspiration, and Motivation.
I face the mirror: perfection.
I AM the reflection.

–Sheryl Smikle-Russell

**Note to self - "How I view myself is how I will treat myself. It is not about what others see–it is about what I see in the mirror, and that is where my power lies."*

–Sheryl Smikle-Russell

THE I AM MINDSET is about choosing to be Inspiring, Aspiring, and Motivating. Developing a healthy mindset is the first step in holding myself accountable for being the best version of myself. This successful action starts with a thought, and thoughts are unlimited. When I focus, my mind and heart connect on a deeper emotional level.

Intentional thoughts usually ignite several feelings or emotions (Love, Anger, Fearlessness, Fear, Fulfillment, Disgust, Happiness, Sadness, Peace, Surprise, Joy, Contempt, Compassion). My thoughts and feelings/emotions are essential in all my decisions that lead to an action step–good or bad!

It is a good feeling to know that life always allows me to start fresh at every moment. But unfortunately, I often tend to limit my potential by not creating the conditions within myself to foster my growth and empowerment.

"Freedom is knowing that I am just a mindset away from deciding if who I am is who I chose to be."

–Sheryl Smikle-Russell

This book is a valuable resource if you are looking to focus on how to work on empowering yourself, how to move forward with the awareness of who you are, and how to reap the benefits of choosing a positive I AM MINDSET.

Here are some of the questions that will help you decide whether this book has come along at the right time in your life:

1. **Are you aware of who you are?** This book talks about how having an I AM MINDSET can support that awareness.

2. **Do you *genuinely* believe that it is possible to have the life and freedom you deserve?** There are tools and guidelines within this book that will assist you in developing THE I AM MINDSET that requires you to believe in yourself and your ability to make your goals into your reality.

3. **What would stop you from being the best version of yourself?** Knowing what keeps you stuck and your willingness to do the work that only you can do to achieve your goal is essential.

Often, we don't take the time to think about what is blocking us from our destiny and why it is crucial to get beyond these blockages. As a result, we sometimes give up when something challenges our ideas about what we can accomplish at first within ourselves and then possibly with the support of others.

As we journey together, we will continue to explore the inner work necessary to replace that self-limiting talk that may stand in the way of your success in cultivating that new I AM (Inspiring, Aspiring, and Motivating) MINDSET.

May I ask you a favor?

Let's take a moment to do an exercise that I hope you will find relaxing. I want you to breathe in slowly and count to three in your mind; hold that breath and count to five in your mind, then exhale slowly while counting to seven. Repeat this breathing exercise three times.

Please envision yourself doing all the things that you believe you can do. (Yes, you are in a good place, you love who you are, you are in love with that special someone, you are setting goals for yourself, you enjoy your work, you are healthy, and you are blessed, and you know it!)

Now imagine yourself being happy, healthy, and prosperous. These are all beautiful thoughts – How did that feel? Are you willing to do whatever it will take to make these thoughts your reality? I want to encourage you to practice this exercise twice daily (once with your eyes open and once closed). Are you ready to continue the journey of discovering who you are? And to claim your power in sharing your story?

Sharing my story allows me to learn from my past and claim my NOW.

In the story above about coming to America, I made the conscious decision to be vulnerable. I stepped in the fullness of my power as a young teenage girl and a woman who is still learning to embrace life in each moment.

Now I am choosing to walk in my purpose in connecting to you. There was an unspoken understanding that life had granted me an opportunity for a new beginning, and I faithfully and passionately embarked on this new and exciting life journey.

I'm learning that removing my fear of being vulnerable (by telling my story) is enough to set me free to share it.

The former me would have been very reluctant about sharing personal challenges. I felt that if I shared the stories of my struggles, this would mean that I was not grateful for my blessings. I would also get uncomfortable when talking about any successes that I experienced in my life. I feared that others would not respect my achievements because I did not have a fancy degree attached to my name.

"Until you make the unconscious conscious, it will direct your life, and you will call it fate."

–Carl Jung

There were times in the past when I would avoid discussions about the size of my family out of fear that others may doubt my ability to focus on being a successful professional because I had a large family.

Sometimes it is difficult to share our stories because we may not see them as being relevant—we may be fearful of criticism from others or even be ashamed of our past decisions. Understandably, we may feel this way—the fear of being vulnerable can keep us feeling like prisoners in our thoughts.

As a result, we can often get stuck in the fear-based stories of the past, unable to focus on the present, which may leave us doubtful about our future.

However, every aspect of our life story is relevant, and it is up to us to share what we are comfortable sharing without the fear of being judged. Our awareness of what we know is possible grants us the power to cultivate our new reality.

Today, I AM Inspiring, Aspiring, and Motivating. My husband and I have eleven children—six of which are biological, and seventeen years ago, we became guardians to our thirteen-year-old nephew. We are also guardians of three nieces and a nephew in Jamaica. I AM a grandmother, a registered nurse, a real estate broker, an instructor in the medical field, an entrepreneur, and a certified life coach. I AM proud of all that I've accomplished. I AM grateful for my journey.

MY I AM JOURNAL

Self-Reflection

Discovering Who I Am!

"Each moment describes who you are and gives you the opportunity to decide if that's who you want to be."

– Unknown

I Am Taking a Ball Dropping Moment to Reflect on My ….

Thoughts……

Emotions………

Actions…………

Chapter 2

The Inspiration Behind

"I Am My Story"

*"**I AM**" (Inspiring Aspiring Motivating) My Story–*

I will not look to the world to decide what it means to be me. I AM – my self-affirmation that validates my awareness of who I know myself to be!"

–Sheryl Smikle-Russell

The obstacles I went through in My Story inspired me to succeed for the sake of my children.

In 2008, my four older teenage children seemed to be going through adolescent changes simultaneously–especially the boys. They did not want to go to church; they complained about not having any freedom and made excuses for everything. Of course, they always said they couldn't wait to be grown–sound familiar?

There was a time in my life when I thought and felt the same way.

I remember I sat all my children down one Sunday afternoon, and we had a deep conversation. Come to think of it; I lectured them on the importance of being responsible for their actions. I made the analogy of me being a workaholic. If I needed help, there was nothing they (my children) or anyone else could do to help me until I was ready to say, "I am a workaholic, I need help, and I want to have a better quality of life."

I used this analogy to show my children that we are all responsible for knowing who we are and holding ourselves accountable for our decisions, good or bad.

I explained that the statement "I AM" is a solid affirmation to self and that each one of us must come to terms with who we are and recognize the need for change.

I also told them that I would spend lots of time and energy trying to block out the noise from the voices of others in the past, interjecting their thoughts about who they thought I was or who I should be. Through this struggle, I made it clear that I have learned how to nurture the power of my voice and the awareness that it is most important to focus on who I AM and what is natural for me.

I became obsessed with finding ways for my children to relate to my story, and I AM MINDSET. At first, I made every effort to be responsible for my actions–good, bad, or indifferent. Let's say my kids noticed that I didn't stop at a stop sign or drive over the speed limit. I never said that it was okay because I was running late. I never made an excuse for the infraction. I admitted that I was wrong and that I had no reason for breaking the law.

Then I would try to incorporate THE I AM MINDSET into every aspect of our lives. Afterward, everyone was held accountable for their actions and reactions.

My Obsession

"Never give up. Great things take time."
— *Dhiren Prajapati*

I drove everyone crazy with my "I Am My Story Mindset" theory. Then one day, I thought about giving meaning to the phrase *"I AM,"* so I created an acronym to provide it with a special meaning that made sense. It took months, and I would spend hours searching for word combinations that I thought would be powerful enough to give the I AM the purpose that I was seeking.

After about ten thousand different word combinations, I was super excited when I finally came up with the words: Inspire, Aspire, Motivate. I remember calling my aunt "Dr. Smikle" to help me explain the concept in my head and get her opinion about my choice of words. Finally, after days of debating between Inspire, Aspire and Motivate or Inspiration, Aspiration, and Motivation or Inspiring, Aspiring and Motivating.

I decided that Inspiring, Aspiring, and Motivating was the winning affirmation.

Even with my affirmation, I failed at getting it to resonate with my children. I needed to find a way for my children to relate to the new mindset. So, I ventured into what became Phase Two: creating and designing a logo for "I AM My Story."

This process was even longer and nerve-racking for everyone– including me. Again, I had the vision in my head, but I could not get anyone to create the logo the way I saw it! So, my lovely sister-in-law San got on board with supporting me in my struggles of designing the I AM My Story logo. We brainstormed for a while, then, one day, I got out my pencil, paper and I decided that I was not going to stop until I created a logo.

Once I was happy with the final sketch– it was on to Phase Three: getting the logo on t-shirts that the kids would wear!

I bought black and white t-shirts in every size, and I got the logo printed and gave them to all my kids, their friends, and everyone who visits my home.

Being an advocate for "THE I AM MINDSET."

It has been over thirteen years since I started on the I AM My Story Mindset journey. I tried to use every opportunity to spread the word about THE I AM MINDSET's positive effects and encourage others to share their stories. Being a wife and a mother reminds me to "walk the talk." I am grateful that they are holding me to a higher standard that I set for myself. That is encouraging for everyone to practice our positive I AM mindsets.

As a nurse, I talk with my residents about the benefits of having a positive I AM MINDSET concerning their recovery. In addition, I support my caregivers in cultivating a positive I AM MINDSET that would help with their often stressful work environment.

A proud moment of Inspiration

I remember needing one of my I AM My Story t-shirts to use for a picture, and I could not find one anywhere. So, I asked my teenage daughter Jordan if she knew where I would find one. I was so impressed when she directed me to look in her room in her drawer with all her keepsakes, and there it was, a ten-year-old I AM My Story t-shirt neatly folded and tucked away. She warned me to make sure that I returned her t-shirt because she only had one.

Seeing how much that t-shirt meant to my daughter Inspired me to create more t-shirts to share with others and spread the word about the positive effects of having an I AM MINDSET.

MY I AM JOURNAL

Self-Reflection

The Inspiration Behind "I Am My Story"

*"**I AM** (Inspiring Aspiring Motivating) My Story–*
I will not look to the world to decide what it means to be me. I AM - my self-affirmation that validates my awareness of who I know myself to be!"– Sheryl Smikle-Russell

I Am Taking a Ball Dropping Moment to Reflect on My ....

Thoughts

Emotions

Actions-steps

Chapter 3

The Power of Inspiration

"Sometimes, we have to inspire and encourage ourselves through our personal narrative. And we start with what we know." — Deborah L. Parker

I AM **Inspiring**.

What do those words mean to you?

I believe that Inspiration is any force that could stimulate my thoughts and emotions, causing me to do something to enhance my quality of life.

Today, almost everything and everyone has a brand, logo, or slogan to draw visibility and attention to their life or mission.

So, it may not be a bad idea to create an image or a standard for yourself if it feels right.

However, there is a responsibility that comes with how we choose to identify ourselves and the value we place on the expectations of others.

What inspires you is totally up to you and being an inspiration or being inspired is your choice.

A source of Inspiration may be through music, art, friendships, romantic love, or a role model (parents, teachers, sports/movie/pop stars, science geniuses, activists, religious leaders, and many others).

I may get Inspired by watching the triumph over obstacles of a loved one like surviving cancer or being the first person in the family to have a Ph.D.

When we feel Inspired, we want to act. For example, we might want to copy the success of others, or we are Inspired to create and achieve our own unique goals and dreams.

So, Inspiration is key to getting us going. It's the spark that starts the fire. It makes us want to search for our meaning and purpose in life, like start exercising and stick to that healthy diet longer than three months from your New Year's resolution. Write a blog or an article – finish that term paper for a class. Or, more importantly, plan a career map.

"Our chief want is someone who will inspire us to be what we know we could be." –Ralph Waldo Emerson

Let's find out who and what Inspires you:

1. What three people Inspire you the most? Why? Is there something common among them?

2. Have you ever Inspired anyone to do something? What was it? How did you feel knowing you were the spark for their fire?

3. Other than people, what else Inspires you? What is it about those things that encourage you?

We can see that there are two parts to the I of I AM. One is to be Inspired, and the other is to Inspire others. So how do we get more of both?

Once you have answered the question above about who Inspires you, it will be clear what motivates others.

"Sometimes people come into your life for a moment, a day or a lifetime – it matters not the time they spent with you but how they impacted your life in that time." –Unknown

There are instances in life when Inspiration fundamentally changes our sense of personal power in a way that opens opportunities and diverse forms of being for others. I have been fortunate to have experienced many sources of Inspiration in my life and have the privilege of Inspiring others.

I want to take a moment to share a few instances where I was an inspiration to others and some stories about people I met who Inspired me.

My grandmother "Sis" was the person who Inspired me the most as a child. Sis was very young when she had her first child. She later got married and had several children with her husband, and then her husband passed away at an early age, leaving her as a single parent.

Sis later fell in love with a new man (he also died early) and had three more children. After that, she decided to remain single. "God became my husband," she said.

Sis helped nurture many grand and great-grandkids. Her life was inspiring to me because I never heard her complain or blame her circumstances. Instead, she leaned on her faith, worked hard, and did her best to support her family.

I lived with Sis when I was a young baby after all eleven children were grown, except one (my favorite uncle) was still living at home.

Sis was the matriarch of our family and a lifeline to many. She was a praying woman who considered everything a blessing and was always grateful that she had enough to share.

My cousins and I share many stories about the influences that Sis had in our lives.

I was and still am a slow eater and would hate it when we had unexpected visitors (which was all the time).

Sis would always take food from our plates to make up the food for our guests. As a result, I developed a nasty habit of stuffing my mouth and then slowly chewing it, leaving less food to take away from my plate.

My Inspiration to be Christ-like, have strong faith, and believe in myself came from the examples of how my grandmother, Sis, lived her life.

As an adult, I taught my children to share and care for others. Because Sis was compassionate, and I thought that it was the only way to interact with people.

"Life is a journey!"–Unknown

That was my mother's favorite quote.

My mom Veronica was the best. She was an inspiration in many ways. Mommy made a courageous and loving decision to place me in my grandmother's care at that time when she couldn't financially provide for me. Although she wasn't the matriarch – my Mommy maintained a strong presence and a beacon of support in my life as a child and straight through into my adult life.

Mommy was a nurturer, and she was a selfless person who was obsessed with cleaning. She worked hard and fed everyone who needed a meal. She always found the time to give a helping hand to others.

An Inspiring lesson about self-empowerment from my dad:

I feel like the luckiest girl in the world because I have the best dad in the world! I tell everyone that I get my calm and patient demeanor from my dad.

I remember as a little girl asking my father for permission to go somewhere or do something – for example, I would ask, "Daddy, can I go to the beach?"

My dad always said, "I don't know what you are capable of doing or not doing."

So, I knew straight away that I needed to rephrase my question, "Daddy, may I go to the beach?" I found this empowering, and it reinforced the idea that I had ownership of what I could and could not do even though I needed permission.

So, to create and cultivate a self-accountability mindset, I would think more carefully about what I was asking my dad permission to do, that I could do it, and that I would be responsible for the results of my actions.

"Be the light in the darkness to inspire and to enlighten others." –Debasish Mridha

When it comes to being an Inspiration, I used to be uncomfortable when receiving compliments about my impact on others. I thought there was no need for praise or gratitude because taking care of others was a natural duty. Over the years, I've learned to accept compliments, especially when people express their appreciation for something I said or did that positively affects their life.

Sometimes we can inspire change that has a ripple effect in an entire community.

My children still haven't gotten over the fact that their mother started a petition to implement uniforms at their middle school.

I was the vice president of the PTA at the time, and I had three children under ten years old at the school. The dress code was non-existent, and this was becoming a hindrance to learning. I mentioned the idea of having uniforms in the school, and the feedback was poor. The principal told me that the school had tried on numerous occasions and was unsuccessful. He said that he would be leaving the decision to the parents.

I took the initiative to start a petition, and one year later, the school had a new uniform policy.

So, several years later, I was at a uniform store to get some supplies for my daughters, and the owner told me how proud it made her feel to provide the local public schools with uniforms. She also shared her story of years of trying to get support for having uniforms in the public school, but she was unsuccessful.

She was grateful to the person/persons who were instrumental in getting it done.

Today all the city pre-school, middle school, and high schoolers all wear uniforms.

I am sure that you have many stories to tell of being inspired and inspiring others. Hold on to those stories because they can be memories you go back to when you feel unmotivated and rudderless repeatedly.

Those stories will help you make those life course corrections that we all have to keep making throughout our lives.

We all have the power to use these Inspirations to keep our plans, goals vibrant, alive and our Aspirations within reach.

You are an Inspiration for others to Aspire and be Motivated!

MY I AM JOURNAL

Self-Reflection

The Power of Inspiration

"Sometimes, we have to inspire and encourage ourselves t*hrough our personal narrative. And we start with what we know." — Deborah L. Parker*

I Am Taking a Ball Dropping Moment to Reflect on My….

Thoughts

Emotions

Actions-steps

Chapter 4

The Power of My Aspirations

I AM ***ASPIRING***

My Aspiration is the anchor of who I AM.

Question: Is it possible to Aspire and not be Inspired or be Motivated?

Turning my dreams into tangible goals—

It is the bridge between my Inspirations and my Motivations. To be Inspired, I need to Aspire. To be Motivated, I need Aspirations.

I always had big dreams about what my life would be like someday, and I would hope and pray that somehow my dreams would come true.

For many of us, our childhood dreams of what we Aspired to become–do not come true. For example, you might have dreamt about being a nuclear physicist, a ballet dancer, a teacher, or a mother of 10 children. These dreams could've become a reality if **you ignited a plan with Aspiration.**

There is a difference between dreams and Aspirations.

A **"Dream"** is what we see with closed eyes, and **"Aspirations"** are what we see with open eyes.

My dreams were wishful thinking that may or may not have come true. My Aspirations were goals in life, the things that I worked toward and achieved with hard work and dedication.

You can dream all day about being a ballerina, but it will not come true unless you sign up for lessons, stick with it, and work hard. The ballerina's dream is just that—a dream—until you come up with practical, doable steps to get there.

> "If you have built castles in the air, your work need not be lost; that is where they should be. Now put the foundations under them."
>
> — Henry David Thoreau, Walden

For me, this dream-to-Aspiration became a conscious transition, and I found myself setting ambitious goals. There was a feeling of empowerment when I put these goals on my to-do list and took steps toward achieving them.

Yes, I had all kinds of plans for my life, but I still had some doubts about what I thought was possible for my future, as we all do. I asked myself these pressing questions: *Can I make it? Can I work hard enough? Will I keep going even when I am tired and want to give up?*

These thoughts are natural and certainly do not mean you cannot get there.

My Aspiration to become a nurse began with me helping my grandfather. My grandfather was diabetic, one of his legs was amputated, and he had chronic ulcers due to complications with his diabetes. I would accompany my grandfather to the hospital regularly to get his dressings changed.

The nurses would always compliment me for doing a great job of helping my grandfather by taking care of his leg at home. As a result, I developed a genuine interest in caring for my grandfather and others, especially the elderly.

I do not remember ever dreaming about becoming a nurse. I just *knew* that someday I would become a nurse, and I had the Mindset that I would be an excellent nurse.

Academically, my Aspirations to be a nurse appeared to be wildly unrealistic – but coming to America inspired me to start setting goals for my Aspirations of becoming a registered nurse. The process was incredibly challenging: it took many years to complete my nursing training, and I took biology three times before passing it (I never gave up!)

> "I have discovered in life that there are ways of getting almost anywhere you want to go if you really want to go."
>
> — *Langston Hughes*

Many times in my life, I needed support as I tried to navigate different goals leading to my Aspirations. For example, I can remember when I felt overwhelmed because everyone talked about how challenging the microbiology class was that I needed. I dreaded having to take the course. But I had no choice, it was the end of the Spring semester, and if I wanted to stay in the nursing program, I had to take this class by the Fall.

Given my history with biology (at the time, I regretted not taking this class the semester before). I was apprehensive about taking this class for that Fall semester. But I had a classmate/ friend who planned to take microbiology that Fall. I told her about my apprehension, and she told me not to wait until the Fall because there was a microbiology class still open at another college that Summer. But I had to bring my A-game because she heard that the course was intense. So, I told her that I would enroll in the class only if she signed up with me.

MY GAME PLAN!

If I failed the class (there was a 99.999% chance that I would), I planned to retake the course in the Fall.

The course was only six weeks, and it seemed like there was a test every other day. I was not doing well with multiple-choice quizzes at all–but I was doing exceptionally well with the lab quizzes. My instructor approached me and said she wanted to discuss my grades at the end of the second week. I knew I was failing, and I anticipated that she would encourage me to withdraw from the program to save my GPA.

Our conversation was about performance, but she was more interested in figuring out why I was failing than anything else. She stated that it did not make sense that I was doing so well in the labs but very poorly in the lectures.

I said, "Miss, I knew that I wasn't going to pass this class on the first try because I am not good at biology. I'm only taking this class so that I may stand a better chance at passing it during the upcoming Fall semester."

My teacher was shocked at what I told her and demanded that I believe more in my ability to do well (a vote of confidence was what I needed).

I was always good at giving 110% to whatever I did, no matter how hard the task. I was never one to give up, so at that moment, I felt disappointed in myself for thinking that I was going to fail before I even got started (this was so out of character for me).

With her positive reinforcement, I worked my "asset" off, and as a result, I earned a C+ for the course. It wasn't easy, but I did it – not only did I pass, but I also enjoyed the class, especially the labs.

I told my stories in hopes that you can relate to the fact that we can all overcome obstacles to our Aspirations.

Believe in yourself. Do not let self-doubt get in the way of your success!

Plenty of people have set out on the path of a dream with well-meaning Aspirations. They sign up for martial art classes or get into med school, and then they start to lose interest. They work hard for a while, but their work ethic and grit start to diminish. Before long, they give up on their Aspirations.

Is that always the case? No, of course not. Often, we discover if we want this Aspiration, we must immerse ourselves in the steps to get there. For example, after taking a class, we may realize that med school is just not for us. Or getting injured in your martial arts class may make you have second thoughts on why you signed up in the first place.

But if you stay Inspired and Motivated even if you don't succeed. More often than not this is the way we find out that a different path is where we want to go.

A friend told me about an acupuncturist friend who studied biochemistry and came up with a novel idea for his Ph.D. dissertation. But unfortunately, the college said no, so he dropped out of the program and studied acupuncture instead. He has been doing that now for 40 years and has no regrets.

Answer: *So, the long answer here is you can Aspire, but without Inspiration (to dream up the Aspiration) and Motivation (to drive your plan), you won't achieve your goals.*

How can I come up with Aspirations that become a reality?

As you can see from my story about my grandfather, I accidentally walked right into my Aspiration to become a nurse. I was doing what came naturally in helping my grandfather, and I received compliments that I was good at caregiving.

Some people walk into their calling–like, for instance, you might've tried out for the track team because your friend does track, and you discover you are a great runner.

First, it might be a clever idea to think about your goals in the dream and Aspiration stages.

You know you have a dream when you have done nothing so far to achieve it.

You know you have an Aspiration when you already have taken steps toward that goal—no matter how small.

Take a moment to think about your Dreams and Aspirations.

These are my dreams:

These are my aspirations:

And this is how I am working on them:

Do you see the difference?

We're often told to "Dream Big," but this can be disappointing without enough support to make that dream an Aspiration.

"How do I start?" It is a great first question. It would be resourceful to find a professional mentor in the field/sport/hobby that piques your interest.

Another way to see how famous people/influencers made their dreams become a reality is to check out Ted Talks, Inspiring biographies, or autobiographies. Then affirm the information and Google their backstory (it is there).

Every backstory you read will include Inspiring ways some people got around the obstacles in their path, which can help you see that Aspirations are achievable. They also talk about how they kept Motivated (we will talk about the incredible power of Motivation in the next chapter).

Aspiring gives you the freedom to set goals and plan your next steps. Even though you may be at a place in your life where you're feeling stuck– your relationship is falling apart, you are struggling to make ends meet, or nothing seems to be working well for you.

Focusing on your Aspirations may be the empowerment you need to keep going.

Now that you are Aspiring, it is time to commit to doing the work it will take to achieve your goals.

I used the acronym A.S.P.I.R.E as a framework that I created to keep me focused. This is my guide for me to achieve my aspirations. I hope this will be of support to you:

1. **A**lleviate: get rid of all negative thoughts, emotions/feelings, and limiting beliefs--this is the first step in goal setting. Write them down first, and keep this list so that you can see what you've been carrying around with you. This process can be intense–some of these thoughts and beliefs may have been with you your entire life and may feel natural. Start with this list and begin practicing positive thoughts and re-enforce them with positive actions. Remember that change often means forming new habits, so be patient.

2. Self-awareness: know who you are, and this will help you function from a unique perspective that will help you better understand what will work best for you. Sometimes you must separate yourself from the person you think you are to stand in the awareness of who you discover yourself to be. Be prepared to put in some alone time to do the work that only you can do in uncovering the gems in you that are waiting to shine. Write in your journal, talk with friends on the same path, keep lists of what feels most authentically YOU.

3. **P**assion: be passionate about your goals, and so you will commit to the process of working toward your Aspirations, and you will enjoy the result. Passion comes from purpose–when you are doing what is natural to do, you will find that you are more present, focused, and successful at achieving your goals. So how do you get excited about your dreams? You will automatically get excited when your new goals line up with who you are.

4. **I**nsightful: Be a sponge: seek to have an accurate and deeper understanding of what is required to achieve your goal. I have always loved the term "life-long learner." These folks are always reading a new book or searching the internet for the

info they need for new projects and goals. The information is out there!

5. **R**esourceful: Find ways to overcome challenges that may get in the form of your desired outcome. Get as much information as you can about the support that is available to you. Again, the info you need is out there. Find someone who has attained that goal you Aspire to achieve–ask about the obstacles they overcame to get where they are and how they succeeded.

6. **E**mpower: Give yourself the authority and the space to breathe and evolve to your highest level of awareness. Do not settle for less than you know that you can achieve.

When you know who you are, your goals for your Aspirations will become laser-focused, and there is no room for distraction or doubts about your purpose. Good practice in self-awareness is to purposefully speak your truth about who you are and affirm daily with a positive I AM MINDSET. Then, tell yourself and anyone else who will listen about your new goals.

Remember, our Aspirations are the anchor of our I AM MINDSET. They support our Inspirations and act as a resource to motivate us.

MY I AM JOURNAL

Self-Reflection
The Power of my Aspirations

Turning my dreams into tangible goals —

My Aspiration is the anchor of who I AM.

I Am Taking a Ball Dropping Moment to Reflect on My….

Thoughts

Emotions

Actions-steps

Chapter 5

The Power of Motivation

"Our deepest fear is not that we are inadequate. Our deepest fear is that we are powerful beyond measure. It is our light, not our darkness that most frightens us. We ask ourselves, 'Who am I to be brilliant, gorgeous, talented, fabulous?' Actually, who are you not to be?" –Marianne Williamson

Motivation – is that force that I use to propel me forward. It is the spark that ignites my plan.

When we feel Motivated and energized, we think of beginnings with confidence and are empowered to set goals.

Becoming Motivated can be a challenge. There are times when we are inspired, and we aspire, but we lack motivation. Life will get in the way of our goals – that is just how it is.

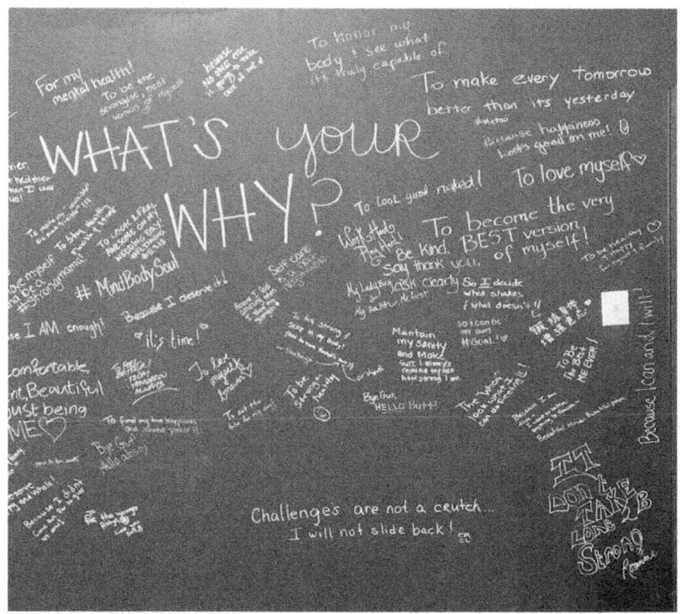

However, we always have the power to choose to give up or get up, which is called our determination. Once you're Motivated and you're determined, it is your discipline that will keep you going.

I enjoy listening to different motivational speakers like Les Brown (my favorite) because he makes me laugh while Motivating me. Sometimes I need that extra push to get moving or to keep that fire going. You can go on YouTube, and there are hundreds of Ted Talks and other videos that can help you stay on track.

Lisa Nichols, Oprah Winfrey, Brené Brown, and Iyanla Vanzant are popular motivators who have been very honest about their struggles with motivation.

Think about a time you were very Motivated to do something. How did that feel? Did you have energy, drive, and excitement about reaching that goal? Feeling Motivated is an incredible force to get you where you want to go.

How do we make that first step into motivation? Sometimes that first step is out of the blue.

What if the Motivation I need is an opportunity that I had not thought about before?

One afternoon in the early 1990s, I was home with the children when a family friend stopped by to pay a visit. He told me that he had started his real estate business and would like me to be his first real estate sales agent. I had no aspirations of becoming a realtor, and he knew that I was not certified. I explained that I wouldn't do anything that would jeopardize my children and their schedule because they were a priority.

He offered to refund half my training expenses if I successfully got certified. He also assured me that I would be able to work from home and work around my children's schedules.

How would I know that this is the right move for me to make at this time in my life?

I was a mom and a wife, a nursing student by day, and a part-time nursing assistant by night. I struggled with being a new mother and keeping up my grades in school, so I had decided to take some time off from school. My husband and I were working opposite shifts so that one of us would be home with our babies, ages two and one at the time. I wanted to stay at home with my young children more, and his proposal would allow me to achieve my goal. That's what Motivated me to become a realtor.

"Take up one idea. Make that one idea your life–think of it, dream of it, live on that idea. Let the brain, muscles, nerves, every part of your body, be full of that idea, and just leave every other idea alone. This is the way to success." *–Swami Vivekananda*

Sometimes the Motivation you need shows up in a way that forces you to look at your situation differently. This new perspective can make you work harder to achieve your goal—and put aside any fears you may have.

After taking a few years off from nursing school, I focused more on my children. I thrived as a realtor. I was excited because my children were in school full time, and my husband was eligible for retirement, so I thought this would be the ideal time to restart my nursing training. I decided that my best option was to complete my studies online.

Everything was great at first, but then I started falling behind on my schoolwork, and I struggled to catch up. I was ready to quit nursing school because I was on the verge of failing yet again, and I felt like I had no more fight left in me.

There was a sense of relief because I had convinced myself that I had done my best and there was nothing else left to do but to finish the semester and walk away if I failed. However, in the middle of the semester, we received a notice from the school that the curriculum would be changing the next school year. The program was adding two new nursing concepts courses to the curriculum. The changes would affect the new students or anyone returning to the program—but not folks like me already in the program.

What if I fail? That doubt swirled around in my head, but the thought of having to take two extra classes was the Motivation I needed to work harder. I devised a plan to make it possible to pass my exams. I cut back on working, asked for additional help at home, got a study partner, and spent a lot more time at the library.

I barely passed my final exams, but "**praise be...**," I did it!

The best thing that comes along with being Motivated is becoming Motivating to others.

It's so satisfying to learn that someone looks up to you and gets their Motivation from you. However, we all need to understand that the things we do or say can significantly impact the lives we encounter.

About four years ago, I met with a group of caregivers and staff developers to discuss plans for a new program. Toward the end of the meeting, one of the caregivers announced that she had something significant to share. She stood up with the biggest smile as she faced me and began to speak. She said, "Ms. Russell, I wanted to thank you for Motivating me to stop smoking."

I had no clue what she was talking about, and I was just as surprised as everyone at the table.

"Ms. Russell, I quit smoking three years ago, and I've been successful on this journey because of something you said to me in our last class," she said. "Do you remember telling us that we can do anything we set our mind to do? I didn't buy into that Mindset at the time because I said to you that I was a smoker for over forty years, and I tried quitting many times and would go right back within days of stopping.

"Then, Ms. Russell, you looked at me with a smile and asked me, 'How is smoking serving you, and is it effective?' So, I asked myself that question every day until one day, I just quit. It's been three years, and I have never felt better–thank you!"

I was surprised at the influence that my statement had in motivating this young woman to quit smoking.

> *"Good things come to people who wait, but better things come to those who go out and get them."*
>
> –*Anonymous*

So, once you Aspire and get Motivated to act, how do you raise and sustain your level of this Motivation to achieve your goal?

Part of it can be making your Aspirations as specific as possible. For example, a college professor friend of mine states that she sees more Motivation in students who have a clear sense of what they want their career to be.

This next move could be developing a plan for your goals, with steps you know you can accomplish. It means making lists—and we all know there are few things as Motivating as crossing things off your list as DONE.

Picture yourself in your goal situation as often as you can. For example, if you want to be a nurse, start planning which fabulous scrubs you will buy. Then, see yourself in those scrubs in a hospital setting, a private clinic—wherever you imagine would be best for you. This kind of Motivation comes from the power of intention. "I will be a nurse!"

Volunteer and shadow workers in that job or do an internship. That would be a fantastic way to see the day-to-day responsibilities and the collegiality of the work environment. Also, seeing people succeed in their careers is a great motivator.

Tell your loved ones (the ones who are supportive of you) about your Aspirations. One way to stay Motivated is to have friends or family on board and to support you. When they ask: "How is your plan to be a writer going?" You will have to answer and assess how far along you are in achieving your goal. They will help keep you on track and support you when you feel overwhelmed.

- Enjoying a coaching session -

One of the great benefits of being a life coach (who supports self-empowerment) is that I share in the joy of my clients' journeys of discovering/re-discovering who they are. I advise them to embrace the I AM MINDSET and use it as a guide.

I use the gift of Motivation to support my clients while they focus on reaching their goals. For example, one of my clients wanted to figure out a new life path after a divorce. Another wanted to switch from corporate life to being self-employed. And a third just transitioned from high school to college. They all sacrificed a lot and made tough decisions that required the spark that kindled the fire of Motivation to ignite and that kept them going!

If we cultivate and grow our Motivation, we can accomplish any goals like changing careers, getting healthier with diet and exercise, finding a life partner, or learning a new language.

Being Motivated and being a Motivator will keep the flames burning so that your Aspirations will get to a successful boiling point!

Let's ***get Motivated!***

MY I AM JOURNAL

Self-Reflection
The Power of Motivation

Motivation - is that force that I use to propel me forward. It is the fire that ignites any plan.

I Am Taking a Ball Dropping Moment to Reflect on My ....

Thoughts

Emotions

Actions-steps

Chapter 6

Being Mentally Strong with THE I AM MINDSET.

"If you have a strong mind and plant in it a firm resolve, you can change your destiny."— ***Paramahansa Yogananda***

I AM (Inspiring, Aspiring, and Motivating) My Story, there was a need to cultivate, encourage, and support self-empowerment. I have discovered that the goal is not just to get to a place of knowing who I AM but also to be mentally strong and to become comfortable with having a healthy, happy, and rewarding relationship with myself and others in the process.

In June 1986, I graduated from high school, and I was very concerned about my future. I felt that I had done my best with my final exams and focused on furthering my education. I knew that my best was nowhere good enough to plan a bright future.

"High school was over! I made it – I graduated! Now what? I must think of a plan," I thought to myself.

In the summer of 1986, I visited my mother and my siblings (like I did every year). For some reason, I anticipated that my visit would be different because my family would be so happy for me. They would have so many questions to ask me about my future. I prepared to put on a fake smile to hide that I felt like a failure and didn't have a clear plan. Little did I know that the best part of my life was yet to come.

"***God** will supply us with the opportunity, but it's up to us to do something with it." –Anonymous*

Up until that point, I had only briefly met my Aunty Joan once before, but I recognized her right away because she resembled my mother. She was excited to see me and hear the good news that I graduated high school.

Aunty Joan was a teacher, so she was interested in knowing my plans for furthering my education. I tried my best to pretend to be as excited for myself as everyone else was for me.

Somewhere in the conversation, Aunty Joan said, "If you only had a visa, I would take you to America with me."

Little did I know that statement that would change my life forever.

At the time, I was not sure if I even knew what a visa was. But apparently, for me to travel to America, I needed a visa, and it was too bad that I did not have one.

Getting a visa was HARD, complicated, and unrealistic. My Aunty Joan, my Mommy, and everyone else said that it was impossible to get a visa–I was young, so I had no ties in Jamaica (I had no bank accounts, no children, and no properties).

I heard what everyone said, "You won't. You can't. You're wasting your time." But I refused to listen, and I was determined to get a visa. So, I persisted with my questioning about getting the visa.

Aunty Joan told me that I needed to have a passport before getting a visa, and she made it clear that this could be a long process. Nevertheless, I was determined to do whatever it took to get a visa. I went to the U.S consulate two weeks later, despite all everyone's discouraging remarks. I had my passport in hand and the necessary paperwork to apply for my visa.

"When opportunity knocks, don't let fear hold you back. Open the door and embrace the opportunity that has come forth."

–Unknown

I know that my Aunty Joan had good intentions when she said, "If only I could take you to America." But I didn't think that she had any idea that this was the lifeline that I was hoping for and that I was ready and willing to do whatever it took for an opportunity to get to America.

I arrived at the U.S consulate at 4:30 AM, and there were 50-100 people in line waiting ahead of me. I prayed so hard that I would get the visa. Then suddenly, I noticed only five people were in front of me in line. It was about 10:45 am, and I remember hearing the officer say the words, "I'm sorry. Unfortunately, no. Maybe next time."

The lady in the front of the line started a conversation with me about her numerous unsuccessful visits to the embassy. She told me that it would be ok if I didn't get through on my first try because I could always return and that it got easier each time.

It was my turn, and I was nervous. The officer on the other side of the window seemed nice, and he asked, "Why do you want to go to America? Do you have children? Do you own property?"

Everyone was right; this is nerve-racking! I kept on praying silently – then he said the word no one wants to hear, "*SORRY*!"

I replied, "I'm sorry – I don't understand what you're saying!"

"Mam, I'm sorry but—"

"Sir, you don't understand. I need to go to America, I want to visit, and this is my only opportunity to do so!" I started crying uncontrollably.

The officer tried to comfort me– he explained that I was young and would have countless opportunities to visit America in the future. I looked at him as I dried my tears, and I repeated, "Sir, this is my only opportunity to visit America. You don't understand that this is my only opportunity!"

As I stood there praying, he'd changed his mind, and the young man told me to give him a minute to talk with someone (it seemed like forever). When he returned, he said that this was my lucky day and that I should return later to get my visa.

I stayed for hours until it was time for me. I hoped to see the officer so that I could thank him. I was so thankful for this opportunity to begin my dream.

The story about getting my visa was just one of the many times when my mentality and mindset were at work in pulling my Inspiring, Aspiring, and Motivating team together to give me the support I needed.

So, why is it necessary to be mentally strong and have a positive mindset to keep on track with our goals?

I understand that there is so much pressure on being noticed, heard, valued, and feeling important. We want to be known, have a brand, discover our niche, or become social media influencers.

Everyone on Tik Tok, Instagram, Facebook, Twitter is trying to define or redefine themselves for all to see on these public forums. They post pics and videos of themselves acting, crying, talking, singing, or dancing. We use social media to express ourselves on this unique stage.

Is this bad? No. There are a lot of benefits of using social media to try on different costumes/actions/philosophies to figure out how to be more Inspiring, Aspiring, and Motivating. We get to temporarily experiment with a vast array of personas to see what rings true—what feels authentic.

What can be harmful is being led off our true path by either conforming to others' desires for us—or allowing the criticisms left in comments on our posts to define us and limit how we see ourselves.

"I believe one of my strengths is my ability to keep negative thoughts out. I am an optimist." –John Wooden

"I AM Inspiring, Aspiring, and Motivating. This is a representation of who I AM, not the person someone else wants me to be." –Sheryl Smikle-Russell

This statement may seem straightforward, but we are all torn in so many directions in defining the I AM. You may be a mother, father, sister, brother, son, daughter, student, athlete, musician, club member, Christian—all these labels can feel like they are trying to put you in a neat little box, and it can be draining if you are not mentally strong.

There is so much strength in being able to speak my truth. There is power in what I say or choose to believe about myself!

What makes THE I AM MINDSET unique?

Imagine having a secret sauce that you are excited about and would love to share with everyone, but you doubt it may be practical or that others may understand its benefits. The ingredients – I AM (Inspiring, Aspiring, and Motivating) are freely available to everyone. Each component serves a unique purpose, but all three must work together for the I AM

MINDSET to function at its highest potential and for each person to experience an authentic transformation.

Let's ask some questions to see how the I AM MINDSET works together to discover and shape your most authentic identity:

We've talked about being inspired and becoming inspiring.

- What do you think are your best traits that inspire others? How could you cultivate or grow those traits to be even more inspiring?

Aspiring is that need to keep going, to keep learning, to keep improving.

- What sometimes gets in the way of your Aspirations? What could you do to move those obstacles out of the way? What things do you do now that move you toward your goals?

We want to be both Motivating and Motivated.

- What makes you feel most Motivated? Is it a person, a process, a practice, or a place?

Think about a time when your energy Motivated someone else to do something that challenged them.

- How does it feel to be able to Motivate someone in a way that enriches their life?

Here are a few more questions and suggestions that you may find helpful.

What habits are essential to developing a positive I AM MINDSET?

I have found that positive mental habits and a good state of mind will help me focus on relevant information. In addition, positive thinking will affect the way I view my life and my relationships. As you know, complaining and other negative speaking habits have become so common that sometimes we don't even notice that we are getting sucked into a gloomy outlook conversation or doom-scrolling on our phones or computers.

It is easy to be pessimistic and see the glass half empty. It is much harder to be optimistic and see the silver linings (the best potential in everyone and everything around us).

How can I live my life in a way that makes me proud of who I AM?

A great "I AM" statement for us to try out is:

"I am choosing to have a sense of responsibility for setting self-empowerment goals that align with my thoughts and emotions

and lead me to an action that makes me proud of who I am." – Sheryl Smikle-Russell

Physical habits are also important; regular exercise, good nutrition, work, and sleep/rest balance are vital to me having the energy to accomplish my goals. Life can be challenging, and we never know what it is going to throw at us. So, when situations arise that need us to be strong, wouldn't you want to be as physically and mentally healthy as you can be to overcome these difficulties? *It just makes sense.*

"Success seems to relate to action. Successful people keep moving. They make mistakes, but they don't quit."

– Conrad Hilton

Having a schedule, a planner, and setting self-productivity goals are also helpful. Staying on track to reach our Aspirations means staying organized (I am still working on being more and more organized). It takes many steps to reach a goal, so we must make lists, set up timelines, keep track of and evaluate our progress.

To be Inspiring, Aspiring, and Motivating, we also must be able to fail. There is no harm in failing if we get back on track with our goals and allow the failure to inform us.

Disappointments make us stronger if we take a lesson from each step backward, each fumble, and we remember to avoid that problem in the future.

After all, Michael Jordan said, "Always turn a negative situation into a positive situation."

Experiencing setbacks are a part of life. Aspiring people work with setbacks to make them into Inspiration and Motivation.

MY I AM JOURNAL

Self-Reflection

Being Mentally Strong with THE I AM MINDSET.

*"If you have a strong mind and plant in it a firm resolve, you can change your destiny."— **Paramahansa Yogananda***

I Am Taking a Ball Dropping Moment to Reflect on My….

Thoughts

Emotions

Actions-steps

Chapter 7

How Do I Get to Self-Awareness?

"The only questions that really matter are the ones you ask yourself." –Ursula Le Guin

We all like to think that we know ourselves better than anyone else.

Sometimes we tend to live our lives like a manufactured *product* – we boldly wear a label that states who we are and what we represent.

"This is who I AM!" we say. (Sound familiar?) This statement is usually to defend a trait that we've learned to be proud of or honor a label that somebody else assigned us at different stages of our lives that never represented who we were in the first place. However, to *truly* get to know ourselves, we must be willing to sit with and relate to ourselves in an honest and non-judgmental way.

"The mind has a powerful way of attracting things that are in harmony with it, good and bad."— Idowu Koyenikan

Cultivating an awareness with "THE I AM MINDSET" is a unique and personal journey. The most rewarding part of this process is that *you* get to determine how to unpack this awareness, how to implement it into your life, and you also get to decide the impact that this change will have on your relationship with others.

THE I AM MINDSET gives you the confidence you need to start an open dialogue. You can hold yourself responsible for cultivating the type of mentality that supports the person you are, not the person the world told you to be.

Start with designing a framework that gives you the mental space and the tools you need to continue the path of fully accepting yourself and enabling the inner work that is yours alone to claim.

Here is an example of an I AM MINDSET. It is the S.W.I.T.C.H framework that you may use as a guide:

Support: Self-empowerment, self-care, self-awareness, and self-love–often, we are led to believe that focusing on ourselves is selfish, so we focus on becoming selfless. However, we owe it to ourselves to create the time and space to care for our needs--this is us being responsible.

Why: There is a reason for everything we do, and it is necessary to assess our thoughts and emotions before moving to action.

Implement: We must hold ourselves accountable for doing the things that we are responsible for doing. Let us be intentional and confident in implementing our goals.

Transformation: We should always have the process in mind from A-Z. What am I expecting to happen due to my actions?

Commit: Be willing to adapt to the change that is necessary for you to attain your goal

Hone: Develop and perfect your craft/skills and deepen your mindset.

Please think of THE I AM MINDSET as your way of defining who you are and deciding to embrace this awareness of self-consciousness. Be bold and allow yourself to discover the freedom to elevate your self-conception without limiting your potential.

This awareness may come from you taking a chance and facing the unknown to have the opportunity to have a better quality of life.

When I came to America, I left my country, family, and everything I knew and loved. I was ready to start a new life, but there were a lot of unknowns. I knew that I wanted to keep the strengths and ambitions I admired in myself and work hard on whatever might hold me back from reaching my goals.

The question I had was: *Do I have what it takes?*

Sometimes, our self-awareness starts with mere curiosity. Maybe it comes from taking a self-assessment test of some type, like, for example, school or work; they have you take a personality test. The result is that you are an introvert, and in knowing this, you should want to know all about what that says about how you communicate, your career choices, your future goals, and who you love.

However, you may feel like the assessment wasn't one hundred percent accurate and too cookie-cutter for you. Some of what the results say resonates with you, *and some of it does not*. So, how do you move forward with a feeling of confidence about what you know to be true about yourself?

"To know yourself, you must sacrifice the illusion that you already do."—Vironika Tugaleva

Often this desire to figure out who we are comes from a longing to question our current reality—a lived set of circumstances that has become uncomfortable when placed against who we know ourselves to be. For example, perhaps in a relationship, you watched yourself speak or behave in a way that wasn't authentic to your core being, and you immediately questioned why you acted that way. You were aware that something felt off–*that something was wrong* and that something was not you.

In those moments, we can feel like a stranger to ourselves.

Now, what do we do with this awareness?

To move productively through our lives, we need to know who we are, and this process may take many forms. It can be questioning ourselves about career ambitions, relationships, goals, hobbies—whatever brings us joy, contentment, peace, and a sense that we matter and contribute.

These self-assessments are rooted in time and circumstance. Thus, our needs and wants change and mutate over time as we gain life experience.

The definition of *self* is not a static thing—but an adapting and ever-maturing illustration of our life. Especially in today's turbulent and increasingly challenging to navigate society, we need to know who we are and our purpose for being here, RIGHT NOW.

Being aware of who you are may mean allowing yourself to be vulnerable even though you feel uncomfortable or even fearful about criticizing yourself. Don't think about this self-critique as a negative thing; it's an overall assessment of where you are at this moment.

You may choose to start by quizzing yourself (and being super honest in these answers because no one will see them but you–unless you want them to).

Here are a few questions that can start you off on this quest for self-awareness with "THE I AM MINDSET:"

1. If someone asked me what my top three strengths are–what would they be?

2. What are my top three weaknesses?

3. Who are my top three role models? What is the most common trait that all three of these role models share that inspire me?

4. Name a fear that I have that I did not mention in my weaknesses above.

5. Talk about a time when I showed how brave I was.

6. If I think about my future dream job, what are three things that position would have to provide to keep me interested and happy?

7. Name three words I think other people use to describe me.

8. Name three of my top goals in life.

9. What would a perfect relationship feel like for me?

10 What are my responsibilities in my relationship with others?

11. What is the one thing that could hold me back from those goals, and in what ways can I make sure that doesn't happen?

Now is always the best time to do a self-assessment and get comfortable with questioning yourself. Your answers may lead to an important question that you would have never thought to ask yourself. In addition, this awareness will help you to redefine your goals in order of priority.

My Goals: How do I decide what they are?

"Goals are not only absolutely necessary to motivate us. They are essential to really keep us alive." — Robert H. Schuller

You may have been thinking about specific goals for years now—but haven't taken those first steps toward them and now are feeling hopeless. These first steps are the hardest, but that's what makes them so powerful. This goal-work is the foundation upon which we'll implement THE I AM MINDSET.

Let's go!

In question #3, I asked you to write down three role models. This question helps us find a place to start thinking about how we want to show up in the world. *It helps us to momentarily focus on people we admire because their attributes lend these values concrete forms before we try them out ourselves.*

Taking note of who these people are and what we find Inspiring, Aspiring, and Motivating about them is an essential first step toward building those qualities within us, knowing where we want to go, what we want to do, and who we want to be when we do it.

The tricky thing about goals, though (and sometimes role models), is that they may often shift or change. Perhaps a friend tells you about a new job, and it sounds *exactly* like something you would love to do. On the other hand, maybe you are already in a position, and even though you thought it was what you wanted, it now seems stale, dull, or lacks growth potential.

Maybe you got out of college, and there are too many options on the table for careers. How do you both narrow down the options and make sure it's the best fit for you?

Maybe you end a relationship, and you wonder what you want or don't want in a relationship in the future. You know you want it to be healthier and more satisfying, but *how do you get there?*

Having an awareness of who we are and our purpose for being here is essential at any stage of our lives. Yes, all goals can indeed be *changed*, but remember that assessing and reassessing these goals along the way is an integral part of our growth and success.

We must take careful steps to develop goals that fit *our* I AM MINDSET when we are walking in the awareness of who we are.

MY I AM JOURNAL

Self-Reflection
How Do I Get to Awareness?

"The only questions that really matter are the ones you ask yourself." –Ursula K. Le Guin

I Am Taking a Ball Dropping Moment to Reflect on My….

Thoughts

Emotions

Actions-steps

Chapter 8

How Can This New Mindset Change My Life?

"Everything is within your power, and your power is within you."— Janice Trachtman

I consider THE I AM MINDSET to be my road map and my compass through self-awareness. The benefits of the awareness of THE I AM MINDSET are endless. For me, the most challenging part of this journey was learning to focus inward and experience the transformation that was consistently evolving from within.

But once I embraced the awareness of who I AM and was willing to surrender to being present, I noticed a more intentional shift in my mindset. There was a feeling of freeness that appeared to be flowing outward, and it was having a positive effect on my thoughts, feelings, and the way I chose to relate with others.

At first, I thought that my obsession with the I AM MINDSET, and encouraging self-empowerment was only to focus on getting my children to be more aware of who they were. And, in addition, I felt very strongly that it was essential for the children to learn the importance of holding themselves accountable for their thoughts, emotions/feelings, and actions.

But an unconscious shift was brewing; it felt almost like an addiction that I could not explain. I embodied a new way of thinking, feeling, and reacting–transformed into a movement that seems to be taking on a life of its own.

At times, I would find myself questioning my newfound self-awareness (it felt like an awakening of some kind, and it was refreshing).

Do I know who I AM? I started thinking back to my childhood, and all the different perceptions of who I thought I was came flooding in. I asked myself questions like *Where are these thoughts from, and why? Was there ever a period during my childhood that I ever felt 100% secure about who I was?*

"The moment you accept responsibility for EVERYTHING in your life is the moment you gain the power to change ANYTHING in your life." –Hal Elrod

My life was evolving, and it was time to change my lens to accommodate the view from a new and very different perspective. I saw a resurfacing of realizations about my childhood that appeared to have been buried deep into my subconscious mind.

It felt like I was in virtual reality– this was a coping mechanism–my way of escaping the loneliness, the sense of displacement, the feelings of not being good enough. I was inundated by an influx of constant reminders of my flaws and insecurities about myself and my future.

Looking back, this seems so silly, but I can remember being very upset as a child because I allowed my cousin to convince me that she was closer to my siblings than I was because I was only a half-sister to my siblings, but she was their full cousin.

It may sound ridiculous now, but back then it added fuel to my insecurities, and I tried to hide it from the world. I didn't know how her comment threw my self-awareness so off-kilter. How did she have the power to do that?

So, this was my struggle—to identify the real ME.

As an adult, I thought I had it all figured out, but then I was challenged to learn that I had insecurities with life and who I was.

I felt confident that going into life coaching, I would be able to fix everything for everyone. Life coaching would allow me to give my clients solutions to their problems. However, shortly after starting the certification program, I realized that coaching is not about doing for someone. Coaching is about ME being vulnerable, honest, and non-judgmental with myself to better support my clients by giving them the space to help themselves.

The hardest thing about getting my certification was talking about myself and discovering that I wasn't taking care of myself. I wasn't getting enough sleep; I wasn't paying attention to my needs, and I didn't know who Sheryl indeed was.

My journey through the life coaching certification process taught me that I felt responsible for keeping everything together. I never wanted to get to a point where I couldn't take care of myself, my family, or someone else. I put a safety net under my life so that nothing would fall through. I thought I had to keep everyone afloat until there was little time left over for me. I told myself that I could come later. I was the wife, and I was the mother, I was the realtor, I was the nurse–I was everything to everyone else, but I didn't put much emphasis on myself.

Life coaching taught me that it was okay to think about myself (it's my responsibility to focus on myself without the feeling of guilt). It was okay for me to pull that safety net and have things fall through because keeping it all together is not solely my responsibility.

I am still a wife, and I am still a mother, I am still a realtor, I am still a nurse, but I am also Sheryl Smikle-Russell. Life coaching gave me support and space to focus on using THE I AM MINDSET to reassess my priorities and some of my limited thinking and be prouder of who I AM. It took this journey to help me discover some aspects of my awareness that needed change.

Let's think of the awareness in THE I AM MINDSET as setting a standard for yourself that only you can specify and only you can indeed hold yourself accountable for maintaining that standard.

How can I figure out where my thinking about myself is stuck or limited?

Here are some questions that can help you see where your thinking might be stuck:

1. *Have I ever stopped to see if any goals I made in the past fit with my current self?*

2. *If they don't–why not? What is different about me now compared to when I set these goals?*

3. *Did I set these goals, or did someone else? Are they what I want for me—or a projection of someone else's needs, desires, or dreams?*

4. *Am I stuck in "but" thinking? "I want to be a nurse, but ________"? Believe it or not—there are folks out there who are successfully achieving their goals even though they have a ton of obstacles in their way (no, butts about it!)*

Here are some of the possible benefits of discovering and setting these I AM MINDSET standards for yourself.

Self-awareness

"I am unstoppable when I am aware that I am aware."
–Sheryl Smikle-Russell

When you are self-aware, you are more focused on personal growth, allowing you to see yourself in a different light. As a result, there may be a boost in your confidence where you are more creative and a better communicator. You may see improvements in your relationships or experience your happiness level increase – with this, you will likely make better choices.

Self-awareness is simply researching inside of yourself to uncover who you are and what you are capable of; this is all about you!

Here are some questions you could ask yourself:

1. What are my favorite hobbies?

2. What hobbies or activities I haven't tried look appealing to me?

3. What do I like to read about? Why?

4. Where are my favorite places to go and look at the scenery?

5. Where would I like to live someday? Why?

6. What are my favorite sites on social media? Why?

7. Who are my closest friends? What makes them unique to me?

8. How would I spend a perfect day off?

9. What current event topics resonate with me? What issues get me upset or make me want to get involved?

10. If I were to do some volunteer work, who would I want to help?

Some of these questions might seem insignificant, but they feed into more important life questions that we all tackle: *Where do I want to live? Who do I want as friends? What career would make me feel fulfilled? What kind of romantic partner am I looking for in the future?*

What do I want to spend my time doing when I'm not at work or school?

Even if we already have some of these things lined up, we have the right and the personal obligation to review our I AM MINDSET to make sure that we align with what we want and need for each chapter of our lives. Self-awareness is a continually updated inventory of who we are and what we want out of life.

Self-confidence

On the other hand, self-confidence is a feeling that comes from self-awareness + feeling secure with your self-assessment.

Self-confidence is the key to success, gives us a sense of well-being, helps with a positive self-image, allows us to see hidden opportunities, and facilitates us to be more productive by focusing on the things that align with who we are now.

Here are some questions that could help uncover how self-confident you are:

1. When I go back to the strengths that I listed in Chapter Seven. What makes these my strengths? How did I develop them? Was it practicing, or was it a shift in focus?

2. What makes me self-confident about having these strengths?

3. AM I proud of myself? I know I have weaknesses, and sometimes I dwell on them, but do I dwell on them so much that I forget what to be proud of and what matters?

4. How do I build my self-confidence?

Self-actualization

"What a man CAN be, he MUST be." –Abraham Maslow

"SELF-ACTUALIZATION is the complete realization of one's potential, and the full development of one's abilities and appreciation for life." –Abraham Maslow

Self-actualization is the key to maintaining THE I AM MINDSET, and our goal in life should be to focus on reaching our fullest potential.

As you can see, there are countless benefits to developing an I AM MINDSET. Having this affirmation in your repertoire as a self-representation is more of a purposeful and positive reinforcement of your self-awareness.

Adjusting to a sudden life change can be challenging–especially when we have conditioned our mindset to be consistent and comfortable with our habits or behaviors. Therefore, we need to give ourselves the time and space to identify the areas in our lives that we need to work on and make sure that we can commit to the process.

Only you know what a life change should look or feel like. If you are ready to take the first step; here are a few examples of ways we may choose to view a life change:

1. A change can mean making ourselves or something in our life completely different.

2. A change could mean just modifying or touching up an area in our life.

3. A change could be replacing something for something newer, better, or different

4. The change will mean we get closer to being the best version of ourselves.

Developing a positive, I AM MINDSET can be a resourceful way to embrace life changes or face the challenges that life sometimes sends our way. We have the power within us to choose how we want to represent ourselves in life.

MY I AM JOURNAL

Self-Reflection

How Can Developing THE I AM MINDSET Change My Life?

"Everything is within your power, and your power is within you." — Janice Trachtman

I Am Taking a Ball Dropping Moment to Reflect on My ….

Thoughts......

Emotions..........

Actions-steps.................

Chapter 9

My "I Am Mindset" Will Be Tested

"If I didn't define myself for myself, I would be crunched into other people's fantasies for me and eaten alive."–Audre Lorde

Have you ever had an experience that put your mindset to the test?

It would make complete sense for us to think that having a positive I AM MINDSET would be all we would need to protect ourselves from being negatively judged or singled out by others.

We live in a society where factors such as skin color, who we choose to love, where we live, our gender, and where we are from–can make us targets for racial profiling, discrimination, and other acts of violence.

So, how do we prepare ourselves to overcome these challenges?

I am learning that there are just some situations in life that I will never expect to happen. But, when the unexpected happens, I can always rely on myself to show up authentically because I know who I am.

It was through a problematic situation that my family and I learned this valuable lesson.

Late one evening, my four daughters and I decided to make a quick stop at the drugstore only two blocks from our home. The following is my teenage daughter's account of the lesson she learned that night.

"We Were Black, and She Assumed"
–Joelle A. Russell

"All my life, I've heard tragic stories about racism, police brutality, and racial injustice. All my life, I've brushed it off—seen it as something that only happens in super racist communities in the deep south. Never in my life did I think that something like this could happen so close to home, here, in West Hartford, CT.

"It was mid-December of 2018 when three of my sisters, my mom, and I traveled to our local CVS in hopes to purchase some hair products. It wasn't long after we had entered the store that my siblings and I were called to the front by police and told to empty our pockets. We had no intention of stealing anything. When the officer found nothing, he proceeded to ask us if we had been to the West Farm's mall recently; apparently, there had been a group of black girls who stole from the mall the previous day, and the cashier at the front thought that it was us.

"We hadn't been to the mall in months, and one of my sisters had just got home from china... That day. Now, even though we were innocent, and they found nothing, my family was asked to be banned from returning to that CVS. Of course, the officers told the cashier that they would not do that, but this experience taught me something about the world.

"No matter what part of the country I AM in, no matter how old I AM or how "Good" I AM, racial profiling is still an extremely prevalent issue in our society. It is a dangerous practice, and it can have deadly results if handled the wrong way. My family and I, although targeted, were lucky. I don't know how lucky I will be when this happens next time–I'm sure there will be a next time."

"With everything that has happened to you, you can either feel sorry for yourself or treat what has happened as a gift. Everything is either an opportunity to grow or an obstacle to

keep you from growing. You get to choose."– Dr. Wayne W Dyer

I was there - this moment became real for me when the police asked to search my children in front of everyone in the store. I immediately went into a calm but protective mama bear mode! I thought, "What *would happen to my babies if I wasn't here with them? Who would let them know that they had nothing to fear? Who would comfort them if they felt violated or let down by their belief that they were free and safe in their community?"*

Why was I feeling a sense of shock and disbelief that this was happening? For a moment, I felt guilty for not thinking that my children could be exposed to discrimination while I was with them. Yet, somehow, I had this unconscious belief that I could always protect my babies from anything once they were with me. Before this unfortunate incident, my focus was only on ensuring they knew what to do if they felt threatened or unsafe when their dad or I was not around to protect them.

"Someone's perception of you is not who you are. When you know yourself, other's perception of you doesn't matter."
— Marion Beko

A few weeks after the incident passed, I decided to talk with my girls; I wanted to see how they were doing. I was speechless when my 14-year-old explained to me about her new reality–she said, *"Before, when I went into stores, I knew never to place my hands into my pockets, but now I realize that I must also avoid wearing jackets or loose-fitting clothing."*

Dear Lord,

I know that this was a very unpleasant experience for our family, and I thank you for your grace, your guidance, and your protection over the mindset of every member of my family (especially my children). We know that other people's false sense of reality about us has no power over the truth of who You have created us to be. May we continue to find comfort in knowing who We are.

I pray [Isaiah 54:17] over my family. In Jesus's name Amen.

I told this story because it can make finding our own true, authentic I AM harder when people in our society have already made up their minds about who they think we are, and we are aware of their definitions of us. One of the main benefits of having THE I AM MINDSET is viewing challenges as opportunities to learn more about ourselves. The ultimate act of self-empowerment is knowing that we can control our thoughts, emotions, actions, and reactions in any experience.

Here are some questions that can help you uncover stereotypes that you may have experienced:

1. When I was younger, what was the most hurtful thing I heard about me from more than one person?

2. How did it make me feel when I heard these comments?

3. Were the stereotypes about me true? What parts were not true?

4. Now that I am older, what kind of stereotypes about me have I heard from my family or friends? How do these comments make me feel?

5. What about at school or work? Have I heard comments about some aspect of me that has hurt my feelings?

It is essential to acknowledge how family, friends, and society label us. However, we must also look at those labels and examine times when we may have labeled others. Knowing how prejudice feels can help us reduce the number of times we put someone in a box because of color, religion, gender, etc.

"I don't want to be fake. I'm just being me. And I have the power to break stereotypes and whatever useless rules that society puts on us."–Bad Bunny

What our family, teachers, friends, community members, bosses, co-workers, and everyone tells us is relevant. Still, it is just as vital to examine these comments/beliefs/generalizations for validity.

When someone tells you something about you, it doesn't mean that it is true for you.

You have the power to reject that label or stereotype if it doesn't feel authentic and doesn't move you forward to where you want to be.

It doesn't matter how many times you've heard it or even if it comes from a trusted source: it still may not be who you are. So, to get to the real I AM MINDSET, you may have to reject some things you've heard and empower yourself with a new definition of who you are.

As the saying goes, "You be you!"

MY I AM JOURNAL

Self-Reflection

My, I Am Mindset Will Be Tested - No One Defines Who I Am but Me.

"If I didn't define myself for myself, I would be crunched into other people's fantasies for me and eaten alive."–Audre Lorde

I Am Taking a Ball Dropping Moment to Reflect on My….

Thoughts

Emotions

Actions-steps

Chapter 10

Release The Mindset Detox

"Shout out to everyone transcending a mindset, mentality, desire, belief, emotion, habit, behavior or vibration, that no longer serves them."— Lalah Delia

What does "Release the Mindset Detox" mean for you?

What if you believed that you had the power within you to create a unique detox that would release all toxic thoughts, emotions, actions and "Set you free." Allowing you to focus on empowering yourself with positive awareness about who you are, where you are, and why you are who you are?

Sounds fantastic—being set free.

But–what if the release needs to come from within and it is deeply rooted?

Often, we are not even aware of the things/feelings that we are holding on to or carrying—like the example from Chapter 8 about me feeling overly responsible for taking care of everyone but me.

"Be patient with yourself. Self-growth is tender; it's holy ground. There's no greater investment."–Stephen Covey

During my training as a certified coach, we attended three in-person Friday to Sunday (boot camp) training sessions. I live in Connecticut, and I choose Washington DC for the in-person training programs.

Attending the final in-person session was bittersweet. I met some incredible people in the class, and we supported each other along the way. Nevertheless, we were all excited to get to the finish line and looked forward to starting our coaching practices.

At the end of Saturday's class, the assignment was to bring something of importance or value to the class, and we had to take turns talking about the item.

I thought that this was going to be easy because there were no rules about what to bring. I decided to take a picture of my family, so I wrapped the portrait in layers and layers of protective covering, placed it in a gift box, and put a nice bow on top. My thoughts were that my family is a gift to me (it sounded like a simple plan).

I got to class, and everyone was ready for the presentation. We stood in small circles and talked to our group members about the importance of what we chose to carry. I was about the sixth person to present, and the atmosphere got very emotional. I remember thinking, "Wow, t*his is intense!"*

I held up my little gift box, and as I started to unravel the wrappings, I could feel the tears running down my face (what the heck)?! I just started bawling my eyes out! Everyone was empathetically silent–no hugs, no "It's going to be ok," they just provided a supportive space.

I finally unwrapped the picture, and I could hear myself saying, "I feel like I don't deserve my family, and I am not good enough," and I just kept on crying. It was as if someone else invaded my body and had ripped open my perfect little box of insecurities that I had buried, and now I had no control over my feelings. Finally, they were released, and I didn't even care. I did not feel the need to be strong. I was vulnerable, and I did not want to fix or control my feelings.

"In the process of letting go, you will lose many things from the past, but you will find yourself." –Deepak Chopra

For a moment, I felt brave—I released every thought or feeling of not being good enough, not smart enough, not deserving, not pretty enough, and the list went on. I saw then that my problem with taking care of everyone and avoiding self-care resulted from feeling insecure about my ability to keep my family feeling loved and secure.

Then, there was a feeling of relief, and I embraced myself with comforting but empowering words: "I AM good enough, I AM deserving, I AM beautiful/pretty enough, and I AM enough." I felt like I could fly, but instead, I took bold steps toward finding and opening every little internal box, door, and window to see if there were any more hidden unwanted thoughts and feelings that needed to be released.

"THE I AM MINDSET Detox"

"Accept yourself, love yourself, and keep moving forward. If you want to fly, you have to give up what weighs you down."
– Roy T. Bennett

How do I start this process of releasing?

It is not always easy to release the things that are not working for us. Being aware of the weight of what we are carrying/supporting is the first step in deciding to release/let go. Building new habits will help us identify and remove anything that doesn't allow us the freedom to be our best selves.

Ask yourself these questions:

1. What am I holding on to that I need to release to be my best self?

2. Why am I not releasing something that is not helping me?

3. What do I need to do to remove these things that no longer serve me?

Here are some Inspirations that remind me why it is vital to release the things that are not supporting my physical, mental, or emotional wellbeing.

I think about the process by which our body maintains homeostasis (optimal health).

Our body utilizes homeostasis conditions to ensure that all the body's systems balance and work together to preserve internal and external stability. In homeostasis, the body's metabolism– or physical and chemical processes, must be working at a steady level.

Whenever a disease or an injury occurs, the body's metabolism is disturbed, and homeostasis is lost! When homeostasis is lost, the body finds ways (signs and symptoms) to let us know that something is wrong, and we need to focus on fixing the problem.

The body's first response when homeostasis is lost is to **release** whatever is causing the problem. A healthy body has a reliable method of **removing/releasing** anything that affects homeostasis.

If we want to be mentally/emotionally/physically stable and healthy, we need to release any toxic thoughts causing anxiety, depression, and other kinds of mental pain. This process will help us achieve a state of contentment with who we are. When we do this, we are closer to psychological and physical homeostasis.

"Some of us think holding on makes us strong, but sometimes it is letting go. "–Herman Hesse

What if the process of releasing empowers you and others?

I like to think of a relay race when I need inspiration about knowing when to release so that everyone will benefit.

The relay race is when teams compete against each other, with team members passing the baton to the next runner. Each runner must know when and how to release (hand-off) the baton they are carrying to succeed as a team. Like a good team member, we have an individual responsibility (run fast and know when to release the baton). Then, a team responsibility (run fast and hand over the baton into your teammate's hand), and we celebrate together.

"When I loved myself enough, I began leaving whatever wasn't healthy. This meant people, jobs, my own beliefs, and habits – anything that kept me small. My judgment called it disloyal. Now I see it as self-loving."–Kim McMillen

Adopting a new mindset can be challenging, but it puts you in the process of releasing unwanted thoughts and behaviors and helps restore you to be a better version of yourself.

So, releasing toxic ideas and thoughts is great for you but also benefits those around you. You become a better version of yourself—one that will be more personally successful and more fun and healthier for other people to be around.

How can I release unwanted or toxic thoughts?

1. Inventory ideas and thoughts about yourself that you are ashamed of or know are not suitable for building self-confidence. Put some of them down here.

2. For each unhealthy self-concept, list why this isn't true. What evidence do you have that it isn't true? When, where, or from who did you get this idea?

3. Figure out some ways that each toxic idea holds you back. How does each one limit your life? What haven't you been able to do because of these ideas?

4. Next, try and determine for each thought why you aren't releasing it. What is making you hold on to it?

5. Now, list for each idea a way you could begin to let go of that idea. Identifying them is the first step and a crucial one.

What I fail to release, I choose to support.

Nobody says that this process is easy, but once you identify these unhealthy and self-defeating thoughts and figure out where they come from, you have made an important first step. After all—they are only THOUGHTS. They are not reality, and we can always change our thoughts.

After that step, it's essential to clarify how the thoughts are holding you back from being the best version of yourself.

Make it very concrete. Look back to times when you didn't try something because your negative thoughts held you back.

Then, why are you holding on to this outdated and untrue thinking?

Is there some obstacle in your way–like someone or something in your life keeps reinforcing your negative self-concept?

Or an even more profound and more troubling question: Is there a strange kind of benefit to keeping those ideas about yourself? An example of that could be, "If I am not smart, I don't have to try in school, or I am lazy, so I can't get in shape."

These limiting ideas about yourself could stand in the way of you working hard to achieve the kind of success you want and deserve.

There are also a couple of other types of critical releases I should mention.

What about releasing a toxic relationship—or just one that is not working for you anymore?

Do you know how to let go of people when they are holding you back?

To figure this out, we ask ourselves some of the same questions about releasing our unhealthy thoughts: Is this relationship supporting me in the direction I want to go? If not—how does this person hold me back? Why am I hanging on? What scares me about releasing this person?

Once you go over these questions and your answers in your mind, you are making behaviors and actions and patterns more apparent, and you are figuring out why you do what you do. For example, how many times have you heard a friend complain about a romantic partner or a friend, and you've asked, "Why do you hang around with _________?"

Only to get the reply, "I don't know."

"We should know."

Once we assess why we are hanging on to an unhealthy relationship, we can begin the process of letting go.

And—what if it's YOU that another person is releasing?

One of the most painful things that can happen to us is to be ghosted by a family member, friend, colleague, or romantic partner.

Sometimes it's not an immediate disappearance but a long, slow goodbye as we feel the connection eroding.

The easiest thing for us to do is to go straight to being a victim.

"Why is he gone? I was a great boyfriend!" or "I have always been good to my cousin—so why doesn't she hang out with me anymore?"

Sometimes we get feedback from the person, and sometimes we don't. When we do, we may not trust that we are getting the real reasons they left.

It's harder but more productive to ask ourselves some of the same questions when releasing those things that no longer serve us: Were there any ongoing issues I had with this person? Did I say or do something that offended her? How meaningful is this relationship to me—and how important is it to her?

Perhaps this relationship no longer serves the other person, and they have a right, like you, to ask questions that reveal the relationship's value to their present and future. It's so beneficial to take the time to look with empathy at how the relationship might not have been working for them.

As we know, relationship breakups are not always permanent. However, to handle these detachments better, we need to let go. We need to respect that other persons' power to decide what works for them.

The more we release that need to force a reconnection, the freer we will feel.

Our ability to release (let go) unhealthy thoughts, emotions, and actions will empower us to focus on our self-restoration work toward a purposeful and holistic life.

Now you are thinking about your thinking—which is the best thinking you can do with THE I AM MINDSET!

MY I AM JOURNAL

Self-Reflection

Release - "The I Am Mindset Detox"

"Shout out to everyone transcending a mindset, mentality, desire, belief, emotion, habit, behavior or vibration, that no longer serves them." — Lalah Delia

I Am Taking a Ball Dropping Moment to Reflect on My….

Thoughts

Emotions

Actions-steps

Chapter 11

The Power of Self-Restoration

"When I discover who I am, I'll be free." — Ralph Ellison

Self-restoration is doing the inward work that only I can do to discover myself where I'm free to: uncover, bring back, renew, or save the parts I feel are essential to who I AM. I get to decide what is worth polishing and keeping – the parts of myself important to me, like taking a holistic approach to life and being a living embodiment of vitality.

When I think about the process of being restored, my mind goes to a calm, peaceful place, and I then feel rejuvenated and more empowered.

To be restored, I must first know and understand my purpose and be comfortable with what makes me unique.

There is a time to repair, and there is a time to restore what is worth fixing.

It's like the television programs where they find an old run-down house, and then they detail all the hard work they put in to bring the house back to its original glory.

I love everything old–and I love older homes! Being a realtor allows me to view all kinds of homes, and my favorite is older vintage homes.

I was in the market for an investment property, and location and price were the main factors. I could not believe my luck when I found a beautiful older home (it was the worst looking house on the street) in the perfect location, but of course, it was pricey. So, we bought the home thinking it would be good as new with a bit of elbow grease.

Repairing vs. Restoring

I remember walking through the house with the contractor to discuss the plans for repair and the budget. Within 24 hours, the project had changed from repairs to restoration, the budget tripled, and the restoration time doubled!

We found hidden doors, stairways, walls, and ceilings, and I wanted to save them all. I tried everything to keep the house's look and its function from over a hundred years ago. It became a labor of love and even though we were unable to save everything, taking the time and effort to learn about the home's history was priceless.

Sometimes when we want to restore, we shop or start a new relationship. But all of us know too well that the refreshing quality of that new relationship, dress, or piece of jewelry is temporary, and soon we are looking for a new quick fix.

"Whenever God restores something, He restores it to a place greater than it was before." –Bill Johnson

Like restoring a home that we are passionate about, restoring ourselves takes time, patience, and focus. However, natural restoration is something that is rewarding and can last for a lifetime.

How do I prepare myself for the restoration process?

First, you might be wondering what part of yourself and your life you should focus on restoring, and only you can answer that question.

Here are some questions that may be helpful when focusing on your restoration:

- Am I ready to put time and effort into restoring myself?

- Am I even aware of the hidden parts of myself and the value they could add to my life?

- Am I brave enough to face the areas of myself that have been broken, hidden, or forgotten?

- Am I willing to let go of the things that are beyond restoration?

- How do I prepare myself for the process of self-restoration?

Here are some suggestions that I found to be helpful:

1. **Adopt a positive mindset.**

"It all begins and ends in your mind. What you give power to, has power over you." – Unknown

I know to some people this can sound corny (*Paste a smile on your face!*). However, with practice, you can adjust a negative mindset to a more realistic one--and perhaps eventually into a positive one (take small steps). Having a positive attitude can be tricky in a social media age, where bashing others, comparing, and complaining has become an art form. It means making conscious choices about when and how we respond to negative behaviors or feedback. For example, instead of saying, "This situation is hopeless!" say, "How can I help to make it better?"

2. **Become well-informed about the things that matter to you.**

"Information and ignorance are like light and darkness... When light comes into your room, darkness must fly away. When information rules your mind, ignorance finds its way out!"— Israelmore Ayivo

Today there is countless information at our fingertips about improving ourselves and our relationships with others, from articles about the newest fitness and nutrition trends and studies to all kinds of fun and serious activities. In addition, you can read advice columns for better relationships or choose to get your inspiration from experiencing life to its fullest.

3. **Trust your instincts.**

"Trust your own instinct. Your mistakes might as well be your own, instead of someone else's." - Billy Wilder

Not all our instincts are right on—as we know from our mistakes. But we are also guilty of ignoring that interior voice that says: "This doesn't feel right for me." I said to a friend of mine that she didn't see the red flags in her romantic relationships, and she said, "Oh no! I do see them and march right on by!"

When we ignore or mistrust our instincts, we may be putting ourselves in danger of missing opportunities for our success.

4. **Be willing to release the burdens of your past.**

"Don't let the past dictate your future." - Bill Johnson

Every single one of us has made mistakes; that's just being human. Living there, in that graveyard of past mistakes, lost loves, is not living in the present; it is not focused on planning your bright future. We want to learn from the past, so look at it as a whole lot of lessons that can help you move forward and choose (carefully) what you want to keep from the past.

However, hanging out there in the past can put us in victim mode where we spend too much time doubting and questioning: Why did I break up with him? Why didn't I study more in school? Why didn't I move back to Jamaica or Ireland when I had the chance? As you know, this (Why, why, why) list could become endless.

Mary Oliver asks us, *"What will you do with this one wild and precious life?"* **This is the most important question of all.**

5. **Focus your thoughts on the things only you can change.**

"Are your thoughts worthy of you? If not – NOW is the time to change them. You can begin right where you are right now. Nothing matters but this moment and what you are focusing your attention on. — Rhonda Byrne

The past is the past and cannot be changed—but focusing your thoughts on positively changing your present circumstances will have a good effect on your future. You do have power over most of your decisions (so make them good ones!) When you find that life seems out of your control, look over all the things you have that you can change, adjust and tweak (all part of your restoration). It's usually 100 things you can control versus one or two things you can't.

6. **Disconnect from the judgment of others.**

The eye of judgment sees at a distance what it refuses to see in its own reflection. - T.F. Hodge

Judgments can be both fair and unfair. It's up to you to trust your six-sense when a critique from another feels off to you. Often, people may be judging you the way they feel about themself or how others think about them. They are projecting their pain or low self-worth onto you. Feel free to use or dispose of judgments individually, and always consider the source's intentions.

7. **Embrace failure as part of growth.**

Denzel Washington said that we should *"Fall forward."*

He meant that all our mistakes could become valuable lessons and course corrections if we empower them to do so. We all fail, and failing is part of building character.

Were the famous basketball players great the first time they picked up the ball? Heck No!

They threw that ball at that hoop thousands of times, and often it didn't go in. But each time it didn't go in, they made a subtle adjustment the next time they shot the ball. Those adjustments add up to future success.

8. **Be willing to ask for help.**

"Ask for help not because you're weak, but because you want to remain strong." – Les Brown

I am still trying to learn this lesson!

It used to be a joke that men didn't ask for directions, but now many strong and independent women feel uncomfortable asking for help, too. There is a pervasive feeling of *"I can take care of myself!"* However, we all need help at times, and it makes sense to ask for it before you are in an *"I have no other choice,"* unchangeable or otherwise dangerous situation. You may find that people love the feeling they get when they can help you achieve your dreams.

9. **Don't forget to pay attention to the present moment.**

"The best way to capture moments is to pay attention. This is how we cultivate mindfulness." –Jon Kabat-Zinn

Every moment we are alive is an opportunity to say a kind word, do a good deed, be a mentor/role model, learn from reading, listen to bird songs, organize your life, call a friend, compliment a stranger (*my kids get annoyed when I do this!*) and so much more. But, right now, right here—is all we are guaranteed, so be intentional with your restoration, be your best self and use THE I AM MINDSET as your guide.

MY I AM JOURNAL

Self-Reflection

RESTORE - Cultivating and Honing Self-Awareness

"When I discover who I am, I'll be free." — Ralph Ellison

I Am Taking a Ball Dropping Moment to Reflect on My …

Thoughts

Emotions

Actions-steps

Chapter 12

Being Empowered with the "I Am Mindset"

"When I dare to be powerful — to use my strength in the service of my vision, then it becomes less and less important whether I am afraid." – Audre Lorde

So how do I go about starting an I AM MINDSET that is authentically mine?

There seems to be a general thought process or idea that we all have the exact needs, and there is an expectation that we all should think, feel, and act similarly. This kind of thinking may be partly responsible for our issues with starting, building, and maintaining our self-empowering; I AM MINDSET.

How do I value my unique quirks, characteristics, personality traits, and goals to create my own "I AM MINDSET?"

Strengthening our sense of self gives us power!

Empowering the I AM MINDSET is both an internal and external process, and I am responsible for cultivating and nurturing this mindset. It is like having a navigation system that relies on my thoughts and personal standards as a compass.

"Be who you are and say how you feel, because those who mind don't matter, and those who matter don't mind."

— Dr. Seuss

Learning to communicate with yourself and others is a huge factor in creating, building, and growing your personalized "I AM MINDSET."

Ask yourself: How can I create a better self-communicating system so there is less room for self-doubt when I am ready to connect with the world?

Communicating is easier and more rewarding when we see ourselves and others as unique, beautiful, and perfect individuals. Even though we may be part of groups (family, friendships, work, church, hobbies), we are not like everyone else in that group—and we should not expect to march lockstep alongside anyone. Instead, we should protect and celebrate our specialness in each phase of our lives.

"I have a lot of things to prove to myself. One is that I can live my life fearlessly." –Oprah Winfrey

It is time for me to be honest with myself, and my first step is facing my mirror. *I had to do some soul searching before fully embracing THE I AM MINDSET's awareness.*

As a child, I thought I knew who I was and what I wanted to do with my life. I always considered myself to be a "positive person." Growing up, my grandmother would remind me that no matter how difficult my current situation was, a worse thing could happen, so I would always try to look at the brighter side of everything. As a result, I developed this super positive outlook from a very young age (it drove everyone crazy–even now).

My life could be falling apart, but I would create a space in my head/world where everything on the surface seemed okay or, with time and a little effort, be all good.

I AM learning to be mindful of my reaction to how others may perceive me.

Life in middle school was tough–my hair was too short, my face was long, at times my face was broad, my chest was too flat, my butt was shaped funny, my upper lip was funny looking, my knees were odd, and I was too skinny. I almost forgot to mention that my feet were too big! But I was very good at pretending that none of that mattered.

Looking back on my childhood, I conclude that my much younger I AM MINDSET served as a protective coping mechanism for my ego. It helped me through the minefields of middle school and beyond.

Today my "I AM good" MINDSET is under restoration, and I get to decide what is authentic and worth saving. The best part of this process is holding myself accountable for knowing what is real for me and freely expressing those emotions.

Being honest is a vital first step in creating your I AM MINDSET: you need to assess and reassess what is working for you and what has lost its value.

These are just a few ways that creating THE I AM MINDSET is empowering and can mean the difference between success and failure.

Now is an excellent time to develop new habits that align with who you are at this moment.

Here are some ideas that may help you start a new authentic I AM MINDSET:

1. Get comfortable with who you are

2. Be willing to change the things that are not working for you

3. Spend time with yourself doing nothing

4. Create a list of twelve things about yourself that you are grateful for.

5. Each day find six things that you are ready to release

6. Each day find three things that you would like to restore.

7. Create a bucket list with at least seven things the future you would do

8. Take 10 minutes each day to focus on what inspires you

9. Take 15 minutes each day to focus on your aspirations/dreams.

10. Take 5 minutes each day to focus on who or what motivates you

11. Take a moment to share your feelings with someone

12. Take a moment to fill up with twelve self-empowering affirmations.

"I AM Affirmations"

- I AM blessed
- I AM positive
- I AM beautiful
- I AM living a life of purpose
- I AM confident
- I AM loved
- I AM worthy
- I AM healthy
- I AM enough
- I AM a fantastic person
- I AM proud of who I AM
- I AM unstoppable
- I AM who I say I AM!

A positive, self-empowered I AM MINDSET will cultivate a positive "You are" mentality and work together in supporting my I AM MINDSET.

When you are actively working on your restoration, you become more comfortable with who you are and are receptive to compliments from others.

Everyone likes to hear positive "You are" affirmations:

Here are a few to practice while facing your mirror.

- You are beautiful
- You are handsome
- You are intelligent
- You are worthy
- You are loved
- You are honest
- You are powerful
- You are unique
- You are determined
- You are ambitious
- You are priceless
- You are amazing
- You are blessed
- You are wonderful

You are unstoppable!

You will feel more self-confident and empowered as you cultivate, grow, and maintain THE I AM MINDSET. Confident people support others, and in return, are supported by others. There will be so many fantastic benefits once you begin—so let's go!

MY I AM JOURNAL

Self-Reflection

Being Empowered with the "I AM MINDSET"

"When I dare to be powerful — to use my strength in the service of my vision, then it becomes less and less important whether I am afraid." – Audre Lorde

I Am Taking a Ball Dropping Moment to Reflect on My ….

Thoughts

Emotions

Actions-steps

Chapter 13

Staying Focus on the "I Am Mindset" Path

"The positive thinker sees the invisible, feels the intangible, and achieves the impossible."–Winston Churchill

Spending time on this inward journey of discovery is our most important work.

Everyone has a different way of coping with new beginnings, and what works for me may not work for everyone else, so finding ways to stay on the path of THE I AM MINDSET is an individual process.

Therefore, each of us must find ways to remain strong and supported as we move toward tremendous success.

This support and strength might come from friends, family, teachers, clubs, or organizations you belong to, meditation, or a variety of philosophical and religious beliefs.

The path of THE I AM MINDSET may not be easy, but it will be rewarding!

"For we walk by faith, not by sight" (2 Corinthians 5:7)

I rely on my faith to guide me through many challenging situations in my life. My grandmother taught me how to live by faith, pray, and be Christ-like. I used to think that how I chose to live my life was just a natural way of living. I've learned that this was and still is a choice, and we all have options, but it's not always easy. Sometimes doubts and fears get in the way, and I must exercise my faith beyond what I think is possible.

I was 29 years old and pregnant with my third child. My doctor discovered that there might be something wrong with my pregnancy and my blood work confirmed his suspicion that my baby may have the chromosomal defect that leads to Downs Syndrome. The news was difficult for my husband and me to hear. So, we did amniocentesis (a test to check for congenital disabilities), and the results were abnormal.

Hebrews 11:1, "Now faith is the assurance of things hoped for, the conviction of things not seen,"

We had the option to abort our baby as it would be difficult to care for our ten-month-old, a two-year-old baby, and a new baby with a disability. I did not know how we would manage, but I knew that my God was in control and that we would be ok.

I relied on my faith and the love and support of my family. I focused on believing that my baby was going to be perfect no matter what. I prayed for a miracle even though the doctors were telling us the test results.

Staying on my I AM path was a journey of being faith-focused.

On June 19, 1997, I gave birth to a healthy, happy, beautiful baby girl.

You can see that my faith, family, and friends got me through one of the most challenging times in my life. However, we need support to stay on the I AM path, and there are many ways to find that support.

Who can you reach out to for the help and support you need for this critical work?

Here are some suggestions about finding the support you need:

1. Be honest about your journey. Sharing your plans/goals often encourages others to give you valuable information/advice.

2. Look to align yourself with others who have had similar struggles but have overcome them. Or think about a previous challenge and how you got through it on your own.

3. Sometimes we can find the support we need while we are supporting others. Can you volunteer with an organization that has goals like yours?

4. Have a friend as your accountability partner. Have them check in with you on your progress.

While it is essential to get outside support, the bulk of this inner work to create and maintain my own, I AM MINDSET is on me. Most of this work is very personal and involves a lot of introspection, so I will need the space and the time to focus on doing this.

For instance, if I choose to live a healthy lifestyle, I must decide what this means to me, why this is important, and decide I am willing to do whatever it takes to reach my goal.

The thought of being healthy may be the **Inspiration** that sparked my interest in being healthy. My **Aspirations** to be a healthier version of myself are the fuel to support that spark that will keep me **Motivated**.

Once you know all the benefits of having an I AM MINDSET and staying on that path, you need a plan to support your unique aspirations.

To be successful in my goals, I create support systems by using things I enjoy as a framework.

I love tea, so I created a **T.E.A.** (**T**houghts, **E**motions, and **A**ction-steps) recipe to help me focus on having a positive I AM Mindset. I call this "I need a **T.E.A** assessment time."

T.E.A. time is whenever I need to take a moment to make an important decision.

Here is how this works for me.

I think about my **Thoughts**: They are there for a reason. What is my intention/end goal, and does it align with who I am now?

Emotions: How do I feel about setting out to get this goal? Why do I want it? How will it make me feel when I attain this goal?

Action-steps: How do I get there? What am I willing to do to get there? What's the first step?

Being on THE I AM MINDSET path requires me to be present and focused on creating my personalized journey. I get to navigate my way by using THE I AM MINDSET as my compass.

Sometimes it will be challenging to be alone while doing this work, so I must be careful not to be tempted to use this time of isolation to look for outward distractions instead of looking inward. However, there is no more valuable work that I can do than to be introspective and figure out who I AM because my future success depends on my current decisions.

MY I AM JOURNAL

Self-Reflection

Staying Focus on "THE I AM MINDSET" Path

The positive thinker sees the invisible, feels the intangible, and achieves the impossible." –Winston Churchill

I Am Taking a Ball Dropping Moment to Reflect on My….

Thoughts

Emotions

Actions-steps

Chapter 14

I Deserve Self-Care

"You yourself, as much as anybody in the entire universe, deserve your love and affection." –Buddha

Having an I AM MINDSET is very resourceful, especially when the goal is to break a cycle that has been around for generations. Most of us are familiar with a culture where we learn how to care or not care for ourselves by observing our loved ones.

Each generation took on the selfless responsibility to pave the path to a better future for the next generation, but this often meant neglecting their own need for self-care.

My mother and grandmother would often go to bed after midnight and rise before the crack of dawn to keep food on the table. Their lessons on survival were from their parents and grandparents, who also did what they had to do so that life would be better for their children and grandchildren.

Self-care meant eating food that made them strong and getting just enough sleep to do what they needed to do to take care of the family. They did not have much time to focus on their thoughts, emotions, or actions towards personal goals.

It makes sense that because we love our family, we are willing to work hard and go the extra mile to create opportunities for their wellbeing and success in life. However, a vital lesson for us to learn is that we need to spend quality time honoring, empowering, and caring for ourselves to show up to be our best selves.

"A healthy self-love means we have no compulsion to justify to ourselves or others why we take vacations, why we sleep late, why we buy new shoes, why we spoil ourselves from time to time. We feel comfortable doing things which add quality and beauty to life." –Andrew Matthews

I don't think any time spent on self-care and self-love is selfish. On the contrary, self-care is the final piece of THE I AM MINDSET which helps us cultivate the best version of ourselves (mentally and physically), so we have the strength to face all of life's challenges and blessings head-on.

Here are some questions to get you thinking about your own self-care needs:

1. Is self-care a priority for you? Why or why not?

2. What types of self-care do you use now? Do you meditate, exercise, walk along the beach, play with a pet, get your nails done?

3. How do you feel after self-care? Do you have conflicting feelings about it? Does it ever feel selfish to you? Do you ever feel guilty about taking this time for yourself?

4. What would motivate you to take this essential time for yourself? How can you make more space for it in your life?

2015 is a year I won't forget, not because I was 47 years old or because it was the year of my 20th wedding anniversary, or because I said I would retire in three years and move to North Carolina with my husband. But it was because, on Friday, December 18, 2015, I said goodbye to my mother just eight months after her diagnosis of cancer.

I can remember everything about my mother's cancer journey, but I don't remember ever thinking that my mother would or could die from her illness.

I am a lot like my mother was–a strong woman. We take care of the needs of others, do what we need to do to survive, never give up, and we're never afraid of hard work. In her time of need, I wanted my mother to know that we would fight this battle together and that we were going to win.

"I am not alone" was a phrase my mother would use as comfort during her illness, and I would reassure her that God was with her and that she was never alone.

We were blessed to have the love and support of our wonderful family, and Mommy and I were grateful. I was determined to provide the best care for my mother, and I wanted to be there for her to help her fight this cancer. I knew that my mother was a fighter and never gave up on anything or anyone in the past. We were a team, and I did not have any doubt that we were going to beat this together.

However, caring for Mommy was a lot more challenging than I thought it would be. Mommy seemed to be giving up on fighting for herself when her life depended on it. I had never seen this side of my mother. I was confused, frustrated, and disappointed when she refused to eat or even get out of bed. I would get upset with my mom when she would talk about dying.

I remember thinking that this did not make any sense. "*Why would Mommy want to give up now when this was a time in her life that she should be focusing on fighting to get better? Why would she want to leave me now? Can't Mommy see that I am here with her?" I thought to myself.*

I was there fighting to help her, but she had already given up–she refused to fight.

Some days Mommy would show a little ray of hope at trying to help herself, but even then, she was more focused on how others were doing instead of her health.

There was a day when Mommy didn't respond to care. Her blood pressure and oxygen levels were low–I was very concerned. I tried everything to get her to feel better, but nothing worked.

I eventually called my neighbor and friend (a nurse) to help me figure out what to do. We had the idea to have one of my mother's friends call her and ask for help with a personal problem.

Sure enough, when my mother learned that her friend needed her, she became more alert than she had been for days and offered her friend advice.

I found mommy's handwritten Serenity prayer in her journal after she passed away.

God,
Grant me the Serenity to
accept the things I cannot
change, the courage to
change the things I can
and the wisdom to
know the difference.

"Sheryl, learn to focus on doing the work that only you can do for yourself." –Love, Mommy

It finally made sense that my mother tried to teach me a lesson that she had failed to learn herself. I realized that my mother struggled because she wasn't used to fighting for herself. She did not know how to put her needs first and had difficulty accepting care from others. She did not know how to do the "self-care" work that only she could do.

My mother was never a complainer, and she always said that she did what she needed to do to care for her family. Everyone knew that they could depend on her to help them in any situation; she inspired many, including me.

Mommy was a brilliant and resourceful person who was selfless and compassionate and dedicated her life to taking care of the needs of others. She went back to school to become a certified nursing assistant– she graduated at the top of her class at age 65. She was very proud of herself for finally taking the time to focus on her needs.

But, in the end, Mommy stated that her only regret in life was not spending more time taking better care of herself. Unfortunately, my mother tried to teach me the essential lessons she was still learning on her journey when her illness took her life much too soon.

"Self-care is how you take your power back." — Lalah Delia

This lesson about self-care was difficult, but it taught me how to be a better me. I now know that it is necessary to do the work that only I can do for me.

If someone were to ask me today the real reason I became a life coach, I would say, "I became a life coach because I was uncomfortable with myself."

But honestly, I became a life coach because I knew that my mother was right about the importance of finding time to focus on taking care of myself, which is the one thing that I can do for myself.

I AM wholly aware that I am standing on a foundation that has been under restoration for generations. I AM willing to do the inner work necessary to release that which impedes my discovery or rediscovery of who I am.

I AM compelled to keep those unique characteristics embedded in the core of who I AM.

I AM determined to cultivate and nurture "THE I AM MINDSET" as a part of the foundation for the next generation.

MY I AM JOURNAL

Self-Reflection
I DESERVE SELF-CARE

"Self-care is how you take your power back."
— Lalah Delia

I Am Taking a Ball Dropping Moment to Reflect on My….

Thoughts

Emotions

Actions-steps

Acknowledgments

Developing an attitude of gratitude with THE I AM MINDSET

"Whatever affects one directly, affects all indirectly."- Dr. Martin Luther King, Jr

I AM Grateful for my village!

We have all heard the African Proverb, "It takes a village to raise a child."

No matter who we are or where we are in life, we owe gratitude to someone somewhere, and we must take the time to acknowledge our blessings each step of the way.

First and foremost, I am grateful to my heavenly Father for creating me in His image. I give honor and praise to my Lord and Savior Jesus for showing up for me always.

I am grateful to my villagers for supporting me along the way.

It is comforting to know that someone always has my back, even when I may be unsure of my next step.

Having supportive family and friends is priceless and instrumental in staying on THE I AM MINDSET path.

I AM
Inspiring
Aspiring
Motivating
my
story
The Great I AM Created me in the image of He who made me
destiny I see in the eyes of my Ancestors who prayed for me
self-affirmation
Inspirations
Aspirations
Motivations
my story
doesn't
define me
life is a journey
I am on a mission
faith is my foundation
Love is my navigation
Peace is the destination
my plan is in His hand
fear is not an option
I am free to be me
yesterday
is history
tomorrow
a mystery
today is
God's
gift to
me

I AM my story **by** Sheryl Smikle-Russell 2018

I AM Taking a Ball Dropping Moment to say

"Thank YOU"

Richard, I am grateful to God for creating you in His image and allowing you to be in my life as my husband. You are my husband, my friend, and my most dependable support. Rich, you are an extraordinary man (putting up with me for over 25 years takes courage). I love you, and I am blessed to have the honor of sharing my life with you. Thank you for being my rock and my much better half. Sometimes I think that my parents (Mommy, rest in peace), especially my father, love you more than they do me, but it is okay. You are an outstanding person, a caring husband, and an exceptional father (thank you for raising my nephew as your son). Thank you for being consistent and reliable in supporting our family in all areas of our life.

To all my children, thank you all for showing up as wonderfully unique individuals.

Keno, you are my favorite nephew/brother/son. Thank you for always being honest no matter what! You are a fantastic person–father, husband, son, and brother. Keno, you are an intelligent and dedicated young man, and I am very proud of you, my nephew/brother/son!

Alex, you are my favorite firstborn son. Thank you for always finding the time to talk with me and for trusting me. I appreciate every moment with you, and I am grateful for who you are. Alex, you are a brilliant young man, and you have a special gift of connecting with people powerfully, constantly impacting every person you meet in an uplifting way. You have a beautiful and amazing mind, and I am very proud that you are my son.

Danielle, you are my favorite firstborn daughter. Thank you for supporting me in accepting my vulnerability! You have a unique way of seeing beyond my presence, and you always know when I am not authentic with myself. Danielle, you are a phenomenal young lady. I am very proud of you for choosing to experience a unique life journey for yourself and letting your innovative vision direct your path. "I see you"–you are a very thoughtful, caring, and reliable person, daughter, sister, and partner. I love you, and I am honored that you are my daughter.

Morgane, you are my favorite second daughter. Thank you for encouraging me to see myself for the person I am and to learn to walk in my greatness. Morgane, you are an extraordinary young lady. I applaud you for always following your mind, knowing what feels suitable for you, and not settling. You are a very kind, discerning, trustworthy, honest daughter, sister, and friend. I love you, and I am honored that you are my daughter.

Joelle, you are my favorite third daughter. Thank you for reminding me that I should always be myself (perfectly imperfect, and that is perfect). Joelle, you are a sensational young lady. I admire your creativity and your commitment to the things that you enjoy doing in life. You are thoughtful, kind, well organized, resourceful, and very astute. You are a wonderful person, daughter, sister, and friend. I love you, and I am honored that you are my daughter.

Rene, you are my favorite fourth daughter. Thank you for reminding me constantly to be "The three B's" (Blessed, Bold, and Beautiful) and for making sure that I am always on point. Rene, you are a very sophisticated young lady. I respect your drive and focus on always aiming for the best, setting high standards in whatever you do, and honing your skills. You epitomize the three B's (Blessed, Bold, and Beautiful), too! I love you, and I am honored that you are my daughter.

Jordan, you are my favorite fifth daughter. Thank you for always going the extra mile to ensure that I do what I need to do and have whatever I need to look and feel my best. You are a fascinating young lady. I appreciate your commitment to doing things in your unique way. You are outstanding, and you are very successful at everything you set your mind to do. I love you, and I am honored that you are my daughter.

Brandon, Sherwayne, Erica, Ann-Marie & Haley – my nephews and nieces/sons & daughters – You are all amazing, I love you, and I am proud of every one of you. I cannot imagine what it is like to have lost your mother at such a young impressionable age and stage in your life. I am grateful to God for allowing me the opportunity to be able to be your aunt/mother when you needed me to be.

To my nephews and grandsons: **Donovan Jr. Caleb, Carter, Jason & Jensen**: I love you, my handsome little angels.

Jme, Hayley, thank you for being so loving and caring. I'm so blessed to have you as my daughter-in-law/daughters.

Santino, thank you for being a wonderful, kind, and caring, young man. You're a thoughtful and kind person. I'm so blessed to have you as my son-in-law/son– I love you!

I am grateful for every part of the journey. I love you all with all my heart, and I thank God for blessing us with each other.

I am grateful to my parents, my extended family, and my friends

Daddy, thank you for all your ways of letting me feel like the most beautiful, most intelligent, and the most relevant person in the world.

I am so grateful to you for always giving me the benefit of the doubt even when I thought I was not deserving. I remember back in high school when it was time for you to pay the fees for my exams, and I begged you not to waste your money to pay for my shorthand and typing exams because I thought I would not do well. And your response was, "You let me do my job as your father, and you only need to focus on doing your best." This selfless act is one of many inspirational examples that inspired me to be today's daughter, mother, wife, family member, and friend. I am blessed to have inherited your calm demeanor and your humility. I am eternally grateful that you are my dad. I love you, daddy "again and again."

Mrs. Smikle (my stepmom), Thank you for saying yes and allowing me to grow in an environment that supported my growth and development in many ways. I appreciate your kindness, and I admire your strength and your commitment to your family.

Charles, Craig, and Stephen (my brothers) thank you guys for being upstanding men–I love you, and I'm proud to be your sister.

Kevin (my brother), I love you, and I'm praying for you!

Suzette, you're my precious sister and friend. I admire your commitment and love for Jesus, your friends, and your family. You're beautiful in every way– I AM honored to be your sister.

Tricia (my beautiful, intelligent, and brave baby sister), I love you, and I AM very proud of you.

Donya (my gorgeous, brilliant, and creative baby sister). Thank you for always trying to take care of me. I appreciate you; I love you, and I am proud of you. You're unstoppable! Congratulations, and I wish you much success as the proud owner of "DonyaMarie Nails Stylist." You go, girl!

To my beautiful, brilliant, kind, caring, and talented nieces: **Abiah, Abigail, Karissa, Mikayla, Kristen, and Zeshawn. I love you!**

I love you, my handsome, loving, and intelligent nephews: **Alex, Dillon, Donte, Matthew, PJ, and Theodore**

Aunt Hermine, thank you for being the matriarch of the Smikle family and for leading by example. You are a trendsetter and an exceptionally brilliant, kind, and caring aunt. I am grateful to you for being there for me my entire life and being an aunt, a grandmother, and an exceptional role model for my children.

Uncle Clive (Laffy) You are the best, my brother/uncle. I love you. Thank you for always looking out for me.

Mrs. Cynthia Russell–The best mother-in-law –Thank YOU!

Mr. Keith Russell–The best father-in-law–Thank YOU!

All my beautiful sisters-in-law: **Avery, Susan, Lee-Ann, Camille, Simone, Sansherell, and Alicia.** Thank you, lovely ladies, so much for all your love and support. I love you all, and I AM proud to call all of you my sisters.

My favorite brothers-in-law– **Jerry, Andrew, Paul, and Bill** – I love you all & Thank YOU!

Uncle Errol, thank you for being the older brother I never had and for being there for me when I needed you the most.

Uncle Dougie, thank you for always being a stand-up uncle. I respect and admire your commitment to the well-being of your family and friends.

Aunty Jenny, thank you for all your love and support. I will never forget all that you did for me as a child and for continuing to encourage me.

Uncle Carl and Uncle **Earl** – Thank YOU!

To my Smikle cousins **Donald, Shaleem, Judy, Andrew**, and all my other wonderful cousins –Thank YOU!

Aunty Joan, Dell, Tatty, and Fay –Thank YOU!

Uncle James & Uncle Errol – Thank YOU!

Aunt Joy & Uncle B –Thank you!

To my entire **Giscombe/Marshall Family**, Thank YOU!

A Special note of gratitude to my daughter **Danielle A. Russell**:

Thank you for inspiring me to face myself in the mirror and to take the time to see myself. Working with you was a life-changing experience. I appreciate every moment: Our 1-1 coaching sessions, Self-empowerment meetings, and especially our fights about boundaries.

Danielle, you have a brilliant, unique, and beautiful mind. This book would not be the same if it were not for your gift of being able to see right through my vulnerability and encouraging me to dig deep and be honest with myself. I wish you great success on your journey to improve the quality of life for entrepreneurs with "The Uncommon Work."

Professor (Emerita) Elizabeth Keifer (Mentor), thank you so much for your help with editing and your insight in writing this book. It was invaluable!

Vincent Bish Jr. (Life Coach), thank you for all the help you gave me in making this book a reality.

James Dale, I would like to thank you for your help editing, designing, and formatting my book cover.

Dr. Hermine Smikle (Aunt) Thank you for setting the bar very high and your continued support towards my success.

Miss Jada Walker, thanks for your help with recreating my "I AM logo.

Joelle Russell (daughter) thank you for contribution.

Sansherell Russell, My sister-in-law/ prayer warrior. Thank you for supporting me in prayer and changing lives with your "The Fragrance of Prayer" podcast.

The cover picture was taken by: **Isabelle Gadbois**

IF
My
Mind
Frame
Feeds
Brain
Food
For My
Thoughts
Emotions
Runs Deep Empowering Me To
Inspire Aspire and Motivate
My Actions Speak Loud
Words Of Wisdom
My Healthy
Mindset
Matters
THE I AM MINDSET

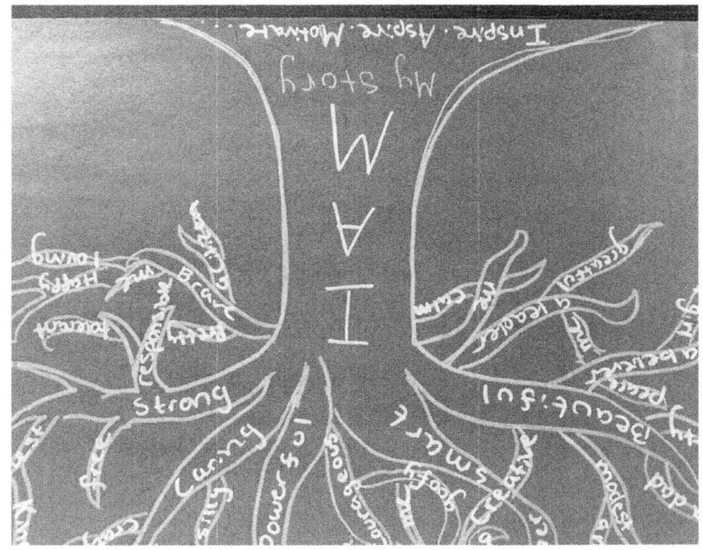

–Joelle A. Russell

To my entire village of family and friends:

THANK YOU ALL FOR YOUR SUPPORT!

To those who have passed away too soon:

Brenton Nicholson (Brother)

Melvina Giscombe (Grandmother)

Nadine Nicholson (Sister)

Delroy Shoughburg (Cousin)

Veronica May Giscombe-Clarke (Mommy)

Gabrielle (Niece)

Journi (Nephew)

Precious memories last forever!

Author Bio

As a child, Sheryl Smikle was a dreamer, and the beach was her favorite place. She would spend hours there daydreaming about what her future would be like when she got older. Those who knew her would describe her as talkative, hardworking, kind, caring, ambitious, and optimistic.

Her dreams were always consistent: Migrating to America, having a large family, becoming very successful, and helping her family.

Her dreams came true when she migrated to America from Jamaica at 18 years old as a young, Black, Jamaican woman with few belongings. Yet, through hard work and a positive mindset. Sheryl became a mother of seven successful children. She's a wife, a realtor, an entrepreneur, a nurse, and a life coach.

She hopes that her stories will help encourage anyone who may feel stuck, overwhelmed and believe that success in any area of their life is not attainable. Sheryl's journey is proof that it is possible to be Inspiring, Aspiring, and Motivating! But your first step is resetting your mindset. "Mindset Matters."

#www.ssrlifecoaching.com
#I AM My Story - Facebook
#I AM My Story Podcast - Spotify
#BecomingS.H.E

Made in United States
North Haven, CT
17 January 2022

14899222R00114